Fred DeRuvo

www.studygrowknow.com
www.studygrowknowblog.com

Why Should We Believe Them?

Copyright © 2011 by Study-Grow-Know

All rights reserved. Written permission must be secured from the author to use or reproduce any part of this book, except brief quotations in critical reviews or articles.

Published in Scotts Valley, California, by Study-Grow-Know
www.studygrowknow.com • www.adroitpublications.com

Scripture quotations (unless otherwise noted) are from The Holy Bible, King James Version, public domain.

Images used in this publication (unless otherwise noted) are from clipartconnection.com and used with permission, ©2007 JUPITERIMAGES, and its licensors. All rights reserved.

All Woodcuts used herein are in the Public Domain and free of copyright.

Cover design by Fred DeRuvo

Cover images:
- *The Book Urantia*, Urantia Foundation (Chicago: 2010)
- *UFOs and the Extraterrestrial Message*, by Richard Lawrence (New York: Chico Books, 2010)
- *A Course in Miracles,* Foundation for Inner Peace (Mill Valley, 2007)
- *What is Scientology?* Church of Scientology (Bridge Publications, 1194)

Edited by: Hannah Richards

Library of Congress Cataloging-in-Publication Data

DeRuvo, Fred, 1957 –

ISBN 0983700613
EAN-13 978-0983700616

1. Religion / Demonology & Satanism

Why Should We Believe Them?

FOREWORD

As I sat down to write this book, I was struck by the voluminous amount of material that is available on the subject of *aliens* and *beings* alleged to be from other worlds and/or dimensions. In fact, it's a bit surprising – though it should not be – that there are in fact so many books available that have allegedly been written or dictated by aliens.

Of course, when we discuss aliens, we are including *all* entities that claim to come from other planets, other worlds, or simply other dimensions. It does not really matter what they are called. They themselves tend to use a variety of names and labels that seem at times interchangeable.

The idea of aliens overseeing and even overshadowing the denizens of earth can be unsettling. Yet, increasingly, we come across greater numbers of people who attest to the fact that they have been contacted by these beings. They also testify to the fact that they believe these entities are not only guiding the welfare of this planet, but state that if we would simply give into them by placing our faith in their ability to heal us and this planet, true miracles would be accomplished.

I have grown a bit weary of the volumes of material I have read and studied on the subject because so much of it sounds alike. The most incredible part to my way of thinking is how people read and accept what they read without so much as a question in many to most cases.

These beings – whoever they are – seem intent on breaking down the natural defenses that human beings put up. We resist what we do not know, and like animals that live and survive by instinct, we do the same thing in many ways. Problems seem to occur when we *ignore* the faculties of reason and instinct. I'm not talking about the way we may *feel* about something. I'm referring to that innate ability that we have within us that tends to warn us of danger. When we override that mechanism *because* of the way we *feel* about something, we are, in essence, throwing caution to the wind.

It really does not matter how something may look to us. The thing that matters the most is what effect it can have on us. Most of us – though we would prefer not to admit it – have found ourselves being ripped off by someone at some point in our lives.

We're going along with our life and we come across a situation that seems just too good to be true. Against our own better judgment (based on instinct and reason), we decide that the situation or the person creating the situation can be trusted. We throw our lot in and sit back to wait for the payoff. Nine times out of ten, the payoff that we expected does not come, at least not in the way we thought it would.

In fact, it does not take too long before we begin to get that feeling (and yes, it *is* a feeling at this point) that something is wrong. Though we try to put it out of our head, it won't go away. Eventually, we have to address the fact that we have been had because we were suckered into doing something our instinct told us to avoid. It happens and it happens often.

The problem with messages from aliens is that the ultimate payback does not happen until after our death. During the interim between today and that day of death, there are things people are said to experience, and they believe it is a direct result of their belief in or association with the entities that have provided them with messages that purport to contain *life*.

Why Should We Believe Them?

In other words, there is absolutely no proof at all that the messages often filling many books from entities beyond our realm are *true*. The proof is absolutely not there. These folks would say the same about Christianity and the Bible. On one hand, they might say that there is no proof that Christianity is true, while other religions are false. On the other hand, they may say that the Bible is only *partially* true because it does not contain all of the truth. In order to have all the truth, much more than just the Bible is needed. The Bible is only one of many that direct people to ultimate truth, but because authentic Christians stop at the Bible, it is said that we do not have all the truth that is available.

But what is the proof that writings like *The Urantia Book, A Course in Miracles, What is Scientology?, UFOs and the Extraterrestrial Message*, or any other book allegedly written and/or dictated by alien life are true? The simple fact of the matter is that though these books may *sound* far more ethereal than the Bible, this in and of itself is not proof.

The Bible has built-in proofs, and because of that, many people simply believe that this alone repudiates the veracity of Scripture. Many prophecies surrounding Jesus, for instance, were written hundreds of years before he was even born in human form.

Can this be said of books like *The Urantia Book*, which is essentially a commentary on the Judeo-Christian Bible as understood by aliens, along with detailed explanations of the origins of life on this planet, the truth about God and Jesus, and many of the factors of Jesus' day to day life? What *is* this book titled *The Urantia Book*? Where did it come from and who wrote it? Does it hold meaning for society today?

What about the other works highlighted on this book's cover? What about them? Where did *they* come from, and who wrote them? Do they complement or contradict?

Why Should We Believe Them?

The natural question for those who are willing to ask it is the title of this book: *Why Should We Believe Them?* It's a good question, and one that truly needs to be answered in order to determine whether or not people are looking in the wrong place for the right answers. If you are one of those people, I hope and pray that you will not ignore instinct and reason, replacing it with feelings and emotions.

Either the aliens have it correct or authentic Christianity is the true source of everything that leads to eternal life. There are obviously many impersonators today. There are many beings who come to us as messengers of light. They can't all be correct, can they? Reason says no. Reason also tells us that there is only one truth that must be universal. It would be impossible to have one truth for me and another truth for you. There is either one truth that is knowable, or there is no truth at all.

You will have to answer this question for yourself. I pray that before you do, you give this book a chance – a chance to help you see that the "truth" being peddled by aliens is not what it seems. Will you do that? I promise you that your eternal soul depends upon it.

- Fred DeRuvo, June 2011

*Listen to Dr. Fred at
Oneplace.com/ministries/study-grow-know*

Why Should We Believe Them?

CONTENTS

Chapter 1:   Drawing Conclusions 9

Chapter 2:   The Earth 15

Chapter 3:   Noise from Beyond 28

Chapter 4:   The New Age 37

Chapter 5:   Decisions, Decisions 58

Chapter 6:   The Conception of Jesus? 66

Chapter 7:   A Young Boy 82

Chapter 8:   What Happened Next 88

Chapter 9:   Mithraism 93

Chapter 10: Death and Resurrection 98

Chapter 11: Last Thoughts About Urantia 101

Chapter 12: The Book of Life 104

Chapter 13: The Message of UFOs 113

Chapter 14: Scientology and Aliens 130

Chapter 15: A Course in Miracles 136

Chapter 16: So What is the Truth? 156

Why Should We Believe Them?

And no marvel; for Satan himself is transformed into an angel of light.

2 Corinthians 11:14

DRAWING CONCLUSIONS

It's so easy, isn't it? It's becoming more reasonable to conclude that aliens, ascended masters, or higher entities *do* exist because of one thing: believing in them means not having to ascribe to a truth that may cramp people's styles. It means understanding that truth is relative, in spite of the fact that there is no way truth – if it is actually *truth* – could ever be relative. I am fond of repeating the phrase that the Bible says one thing or it says nothing, and I'm not the first one to ever make that statement. It is just as profound to state that truth is absolute or there is no such thing as truth. The idea of truth being relative is ridiculous. If truth was actually relative, it fails to be truth.

When people say that truth is relative, they are not speaking of authentic truth. They are merely speaking of something *they* consider to be truth. Because someone else might have a different opinion about their truth, it is understood that one person's truth is not necessarily another person's truth.

For all the supposed intelligence in the world, there is something terribly wrong with that sentiment. Either there is *one overarching truth*, or there is no such thing as any type of truth. It is honestly that simple.

A growing number of people are coming to believe that aliens have provided us with truth. This brand of truth is easy to digest. It is not at all cumbersome, nor is it difficult to appreciate. In fact, the truth that aliens bandy around is like the baseball cap that fits everyone. The one-size-fits-all hat is made so by a simple adjustment in the back of the hat. Simply make the hat larger or smaller by adjusting the strap and wear it comfortably. It's the same hat, but everyone can wear it, and it fits comfortably on each person's head because of its ability to *shapeshift* or adjust itself to that person's head without being uncomfortable at all.

Put simply, an adjustable cap conforms *itself* to each person's head, not the other way around. Christianity, on the other hand, is said to be something that people must conform *to* (as if it is done in the person's own strength) and that can be an uncomfortable process. This is not to say that salvation itself is uncomfortable. It is to say that the process stemming from salvation can be uncomfortable at times due to the necessary growth that the indwelling Holy Spirit creates within the person.

Why Should We Believe Them?

The Holy Spirit's ultimate goal is to recreate us into the image of Jesus' personality. To accomplish this, there are times of growing pains and discomfort due to having to rid ourselves of the things that keep us bound and determined to live a life separate from God.

God does not want us to fail, and He won't allow it; though it will certainly feel as though we are failing from time to time because of what He must accomplish within us. This does not bode well for average individuals who see themselves as independent from God (if He actually exists, they would say). For them, god is within them already and they must simply learn to unleash or release that inner deity.

What they fail to see is that this too is a process; however, the immediate rewards may seem to people like this to almost be effervescent! They often speak of coming alive, of loving others more than they thought possible. They tell tales of traveling through space while out of body, or overcoming the types of feelings and doubts that nothing ever allowed them to do before.

In some ways, then, the body of beliefs bound up within the teachings of many of these alien beings is certainly reminiscent of authentic Christianity with one large *exception*. In Christianity, I answer to the God of all – the very God of the universe which He Himself created. As a follower of Jesus, I am positioned to answer to Him and my life is no longer my own. I am to live my daily life submitting to Him in order that His will, His purposes, and His desires be fulfilled in and through me in order that He would receive all the glory.

In order to do that, there must be a daily battle with my ever-present sin nature that seeks its own way. The sin nature that exists within me exists to please itself. If given the chance, it will live for itself and live in complete and utter rebellion to God.

The person who reads, digests, and believes what aliens teach believes that they have removed the medieval quirks of the concept of the sin nature from the equation. The entire idea of having a sin nature is literally put out to pasture and disposed of forever. It does not enter the equation, and the person who has come to believe the messages of aliens believes they have come in contact with absolute truth. It is this truth that they believe frees them from the confines of immoderate thinking where sin is concerned. Sin ceases to exist, and because of that, the God of the Bible no longer exists.

Gone are the shackles that have bound them to their own destructiveness. They are now free to enjoy life because they can now enjoy the very things that the Bible calls sin. It's no longer rebellion to do what they do. It's freedom. It's maturity. It's living life without shackles.

This new freedom becomes the truth that guides these people, and it is this truth they seek because of how it makes them *feel*. Any misgivings they might have are vanquished and they give themselves over to the full flavor of freedom that this truth grants.

Who does not want to be free? Who does not want to be unburdened? Who does not want to live forever?

The Urantia Book, as well as numerous other books, purports to tell us the truth. They provide us with insight that will bring us out into freedom from the prison of uncertainty.

It is my belief that the entities behind all of these so-called works of truth are nothing but demons that have every intention of deceiving as many people as possible with their ethereal language and Sci-Fi code. They are not interested in saving us from ourselves. They wish to enslave us so that we will not only be no good to ourselves, but will allow them to gain enough momentum so that they will be able to spill out onto this world.

But why would they want to do that? Well, if we take their word for things, they are here only to help. If we take the Bible's word for it, it quickly becomes clear that there is an enemy of man, and that enemy is far superior in more ways than we can count. Because he wishes to enslave us, he will do whatever it takes to make sure that we do not see his true motives. Once his ulterior motives are seen, his mask comes off and he can no longer deceive.

The crux of the problem lies in how we perceive what we are being told. There are essentially only two sources for all information. Either it comes from the God of the Bible, or it comes from the god of this world. If it arrives to us from the God of the Bible, it should be received without hesitation, regardless of how much of it we understand at the time. If it comes from the god of this world, no part of it should be accepted, even if we understand all of it.

The god of this world has one design and that design is simple. He seeks to enslave so that we will be destroyed. It is the oldest con and he is the greatest con artist.

We read all the time about how one person or another was "taken" in a con and went on to lose thousands, or even their entire life savings. How can this happen, we wonder? It happens because people buy into a bill of goods that is nothing more than fool's gold. We were sucker-punched in the Garden of Eden and we have been continually sucker-punched. Instead of recognizing it and moving away from it, we simply allow the process to be repeated, and each time we are conned, we react in surprise. Yet, we do not learn from it. Why is that?

The reason we do not learn from it has everything to do with our pride. We are not interested in admitting to ourselves that we are weak and capable of being deceived and cheated by ultra-intelligent beings from other worlds or other dimensions. The very idea that entities exist who would harm us is something we cannot bring ourselves to admit. It is too foreign. It is a holdover from the Dark Ages. Surely, as intelligent as man has become (we think), our intelligence is miniscule compared to the super intelligence of beings from other dimensions. To believe that those beings would harm us is something that goes against the grain of reason, we think. After all, they are so far advanced from us that war no longer exists for them, we believe. If war no longer exists, then they must have found a way to truly co-exist with all races and cultures that so far has escaped our ability to do so here on earth.

Because they want to break into our world to save us from destruction, that alone is reason enough to believe that these beings are completely altruistic in nature. The idea that they instead desire to deceive or harm us has to be totally foreign to them, we reason, and to think that of them is to insult and offend them to the highest degree!

The problem is that this line of thinking may well be extremely naïve. The belief that super-beings cannot succumb to war-like thinking or the desire to overcome others is merely something we *believe* about them because it is what they *tell* us. Apart from this, there is no proof of their alleged altruism.

What is in store for this planet? What can we expect for humanity if we continue to open up our brains and, more importantly, our hearts (feelings)? Will we wind up on the receiving end of good things, or will we become the target of what turns out to be their evil machinations? It has to be one or the other, but before you decide that these beings are not malevolent, please take the time to finish reading this book. By doing so, the shackles you might unlock may be your own.

THE EARTH

U rantia is the earth. At least, this is what aliens have told us. Our planet is called earth by these individuals. So the title of the book literally means *The Earth Book*. *The Urantia Book* is a book that in many ways *represents* the Bible for those within aspects of the New Age movement. The interior pages are very reminiscent of the type of paper used when printing Christian Bibles. The byline on the cover claims that the book reveals "*the Mysteries of God, the Universe, Jesus, and Ourselves,*" and it does so quite in-depth.

As preparation for this book, I've been reading sections of *The Urantia Book* as well as other esoteric writings that have been written by alleged angels, archangels, and other divine spirits of a sort. It has always been fascinating to me to read what some other-worldly spirit says about God, Jesus, and the Creation, as well as any number of things.

The book can be read online or a printed copy can be ordered. Frankly, I like having actual copies of books to read through so that I can make notes in the margins and highlight to my heart's content. Of course, having a book available online makes it that much easier to pull quotes from, as I've done below.

The Urantia Book

The Urantia Book is nearly 2,100 pages in length, so it's not something that you sit down in one evening and read through. It takes time to read and digest it in order to understand the message contained within it.

The book is divided into four sections (not counting the "front matter"), with each section having numerous chapters, or "papers."

The four sections of *The Urantia Book* are as follows:

- The Central and Superuniverses
- The Local Universe
- The History of Urantia
- The Life and Teachings of Jesus

As an example, the individual chapters (or *papers*) under section four, *The Life and Teachings of Jesus,* are as follows:

- Paper 120 - The Bestowal of Michael on Urantia
- Paper 121 - The Times of Michael's Bestowal
- Paper 122 - Birth and Infancy of Jesus
- Paper 123 - The Early Childhood of Jesus
- Paper 124 - The Later Childhood of Jesus
- Paper 125 - Jesus at Jerusalem
- Paper 126 - The Two Crucial Years
- Paper 127 - The Adolescent Years
- Paper 128 - Jesus' Early Manhood
- Paper 129 - The Later Adult Life of Jesus
- Paper 130 - On the Way to Rome
- Paper 131 - The World's Religions
- Paper 132 - The Sojourn at Rome
- Paper 133 - The Return from Rome
- Paper 134 - The Transition Years
- Paper 135 - John the Baptist
- Paper 136 - Baptism and The Forty Days
- Paper 137 - Tarrying Time in Galilee
- Paper 138 - Training the Kingdom's Messengers
- Paper 139 - The Twelve Apostles
- Paper 140 - The Ordination of the Twelve
- Paper 141 - Beginning the Public Work
- Paper 142 - The Passover at Jerusalem
- Paper 143 - Going Through Samaria
- Paper 144 - At Gilboa and in the Decapolis
- Paper 145 - Four Eventful Days at Capernaum
- Paper 146 - First Preaching Tour of Galilee
- Paper 147 - The Interlude Visit to Jerusalem
- Paper 148 - Training Evangelists at Bethsaida
- Paper 149 - The Second Preaching Tour
- Paper 150 - The Third Preaching Tour
- Paper 151 - Tarrying and Teaching by the Seaside

- Paper 152 - Events Leading up to the Capernaum Crisis
- Paper 153 - The Crisis at Capernaum
- Paper 154 - Last Days at Capernaum
- Paper 155 - Fleeing Through Northern Galilee
- Paper 156 - The Sojourn at Tyre and Sidon
- Paper 157 - At Caesarea-Philippi
- Paper 158 - The Mount of Transfiguration
- Paper 159 - The Decapolis Tour
- Paper 160 - Rodan of Alexandria
- Paper 161 - Further Discussions with Rodan
- Paper 162 - At the Feast of Tabernacles
- Paper 163 - Ordination of the Seventy at Magadan
- Paper 164 - At the Feast of Dedication
- Paper 165 - The Perean Mission Begins
- Paper 166 - Last Visit to Northern Perea
- Paper 167 - The Visit to Philadelphia
- Paper 168 - The Resurrection of Lazarus
- Paper 169 - Last Teaching at Pella
- Paper 170 - The Kingdom of Heaven
- Paper 171 - On the way to Jerusalem
- Paper 172 - Going into Jerusalem
- Paper 173 - Monday in Jerusalem
- Paper 174 - Tuesday Morning in the Temple
- Paper 175 - The Last Temple Discourse
- Paper 176 - Tuesday Evening on Mount Olivet
- Paper 177 - Wednesday, the Rest Day
- Paper 178 - Last Day at the Camp
- Paper 179 - The Last Supper
- Paper 180 - The Farewell Discourse
- Paper 181 - Final Admonitions and Warnings
- Paper 182 - In Gethsemane
- Paper 183 - The Betrayal and Arrest of Jesus

- Paper 184 - Before the Sanhedrin Court
- Paper 185 - The Trial Before Pilate
- Paper 186 - Just Before the Crucifixion
- Paper 187 - The Crucifixion
- Paper 188 - The Time of the Tomb
- Paper 189 - The Resurrection
- Paper 190 - Morontia Appearances of Jesus
- Paper 191 - Appearances to the Apostles and Other Leaders
- Paper 192 - Appearances in Galilee
- Paper 193 - Final Appearances and Ascension
- Paper 194 - Bestowal of the Spirit of Truth
- Paper 195 - After Pentecost
- Paper 196 - The Faith of Jesus

What of course is fascinating is the fact that so many areas of Jesus' life are touched on in some detail within *The Urantia Book*. Simply due to the detail and depth alone, it would be difficult for the average person to set this book aside as something crafted specifically to deceive people. There is too much intelligence, seeming insider knowledge, and too many elements about Jesus alone for that to be the case.

However, it must be asked whether or not these presented details about Jesus are, in fact, true? How can we even begin to determine that? There is only one way, and that is by comparing the pages of *The Urantia Book* to the pages of the Bible. That may seem like going backwards to many who are familiar with Urantia, but that is likely only due to perspective – *their* perspective.

While Urantia purports to present truth and valuable facts about the life of Jesus, can those facts be verified? The Bible is not only filled with information about God, how He formed the earth and created all things in it, but it also contains a good deal of information on Jesus, His life, His ministry, death, and resurrection. One of the most interesting aspects of the Bible is found in its multitude of prophetic discourse, much of it related directly to Jesus.

Since the Bible is its own best proof of its truthfulness, one would expect the same of Urantia. Is this the case? We will endeavor to determine the answer to that question.

For now, understand that the book is said to have come to us through a process of filtering down from the "Father," with permission being given for the Urantia "papers" to be given to us. Ultimately, these papers *"were sponsored, formulated, and put into English by a high commission consisting of twenty-four Orvonton administrators acting in accordance with a mandate issued by the Ancients of Days of Uversa directing that we should do this on Urantia, 606 of Satania, in Norlatiadek of Nebadon, in the year A.D. 1934."*[1]

We also learn that intermediaries were used to bring this information to earthlings. This is a matter of course, as explained by the individuals ("ascended masters") who ultimately got this book in our hands. There are quite a few individuals who had a hand in producing this book. I'm not referring to human beings who physically printed the book itself. I'm referring to those other-worldly entities that are credited with either preparing the individual papers or gathering the information for dissemination in *The Urantia Book*.

There are many alleged entities that are said to have been behind the writing or production of this book. Those who are credited with bringing this book to us from beyond our realms are as follows:

- Divine Counselor
- Universal Censor
- Perfector of Wisdom

---

[1] http://www.urantia.org/en/urantia-book/faqs/how-did-urantia-papers-come-be

- Mighty Messenger
- One High in Authority
- One Without Name and Number
- Chief of Archangels
- Vorondadek Son
- Brilliant Evening Star
- Melchizedek
- Archangel
- Malavatia Melchizedek
- Secondary Lanonandek
- Manovandet Melchizedek
- Machiventa Melchizedek
- Life Carrier
- Solonia
- Chief of Seraphim
- Chief of Midwayers
- Solitary Messenger
- Chief of Evening Stars
- Mantutia Melchizedek
- Midwayer Commission

It is interesting to note that the last entity(ies) noted – Midwayer Commission – were responsible for bringing to us the information related to Jesus. In referencing and discussing *The Urantia Book*, we will spend much of the time dissecting their teaching related to Jesus, since He is the supreme and central figure of Christianity.

In many ways, the book reads much like the Bible, yet is mixed with a Sci-Fi flavor throughout. Here is a sample quote from the first section of the book, and it gives an idea of just how information is put across to the reader:

"*THE Eternal Son is the perfect and final expression of the "first" personal and absolute concept of the Universal Father. Accordingly, when-*

ever and however the Father personally and absolutely expresses himself, he does so through his Eternal Son, who ever has been, now is, and ever will be, the living and divine Word. And this Eternal Son is residential at the center of all things, in association with, and immediately enshrouding the personal presence of, the Eternal and Universal Father. (73.2) 6:0.2 We speak of God's "first" thought and allude to an impossible time origin of the Eternal Son for the purpose of gaining access to the thought channels of the human intellect. Such distortions of language represent our best efforts at contact-compromise with the time-bound minds of mortal creatures. In the sequential sense the Universal Father never could have had a first thought, nor could the Eternal Son ever have had a beginning. But I was instructed to portray the realities of eternity to the time-limited minds of mortals by such symbols of thought and to designate the relationships of eternity by such time concepts of sequentiality."[2]

It always amazes me that for the most part, these "ascended masters" speak in such an ethereal way. Of course, that adds to their mystique. Take for instance the statement "*We speak of God's "first" thought and allude to an impossible time origin of the Eternal Son for the purpose of gaining access to the thought channels of the human intellect.*" The idea here is that these entities have tried to bring their language down to our limited and finite understanding. The concept is that it is too difficult to use eternal terms when speaking of the Eternal Son, so it is necessary to put things into our perspective.

Their use of the term "*first*" is so that people will gain some sense of what they are saying. The phrase, "*...for the purpose of gaining access to the **thought channels of the human intellect***" is simply another way of referring to "*thinking.*" Stating it that way certainly provides an air of eruditeness and, some might even say, brilliance. However,

---

[2] http://www.urantia.org/en/urantia-book-standardized/paper-6-eternal-son

the speech to me comes across as somewhat stilted and even affected. Certainly, one would think that aliens and other-worldly entities would be able to speak as we speak, though that would quite possibly burst the bubble.

For the average person, reading something like what has just been quoted makes it somewhat difficult to plow through, and because of that, they intuitively feel that it must be true.

Again, one would think that if these super-brilliant individuals from other worlds were truly as brilliant as they tend to appear or sound, they would be intelligent enough to speak using far less sophisticated speech. We're not living in the Victorian Era, or in the 1600s when "thine," "thee," and "thou" were the norm. Imagine meeting aliens or beings from other dimensions who spoke just as we speak. That would take away from the perception they are desperately trying to create, wouldn't it?

As you read through this book, I'll be referencing information from other books as well. *The Book of Life,* for instance, said to have been transcribed by Archangel Michael, is one such book. One of things that he tells us is that religion has essentially been a lie perpetrated by the enemy. He tells us that the lie began in the beginning with Adam and Eve, and that the God of the Old Testament – "El" – is actually female. We'll delve into that as well, comparing those claims with the claims from *The Urantia Book*. Do they gel? Do they contradict?

Another book I've been reading is called *UFOs and the Extraterrestrial Message* by Richard Lawrence. The idea that intuition plays a greater part in determining the validity and truthfulness of something is clear in his writing as well. Intuition is of course based to some degree on how one feels about something. In essence, someone who determines truth based on intuition relies on nothing but how they see it. If a person *feels* it inside, then it must be true. The word literally means "*direct perception of truth, fact, etc., independent of any reasoning process; immediate apprehension."*[3] This is in contrast to *instinct*, which is simply an innate reaction to some other stimulus.

Animals live by instinct. They avoid being killed or eaten by a predator based on their instinctive ability. Obviously, it does not work all the time, because some animals get eaten; but by and large, instinct is what motivates most animal behavior, though they can certainly learn specific behaviors as well.

It is often said that people have a flight or fight mechanism that is somewhat instinctual. When faced with certain situations, our natural instincts take over and we often find ourselves doing things as a reaction to something without thinking about it. This is different than *intuition* in the sense that intuition is far more cognitive and parallels *reasoning*.

In all respects, these books come from the perspective that the New Age, UFOs, Aliens, angels and other-worldly or other-dimensional beings are here to present truth, and as such, we should listen and obey. We should not take the time to question motivation because it is a waste of very valuable time. We must get beyond the desire to question and simply do what is being told to us. Though this may appear to be the right thing to do (from the perspective of those beings beyond our world), the reality is that once we stop questioning, we cease to be human. We become little better than animals that live by instinct. At that point, we simply *do* because that is what we are told. We do not question, but simply *respond*, and we respond in the way that the entities want us to respond. After all, they are claiming to tell us things that will save us and our planet. Why should we not listen to them? Why should we take the time to ask questions or debate, because every moment is too important to waste. We need to

---

[3] http://dictionary.reference.com/browse/intuition

throw caution to the wind and simply accept what is presented to us as truth. Don't question. Do. Don't doubt. Believe. Don't resist. Give in. Don't rebel. Follow.

You may be asking yourself, why is a guy who purports to be a Christian spending his time reading books that may very well teach against orthodox Christianity? That's a good question. The reality is that much can be gained by understanding what those outside of orthodox Christianity are being taught. A good deal of verbiage within these books is reminiscent of Christianity. Much of it sounds truthful.

What I will be doing from time to time here is taking what is written in these books and simply holding them up to Scripture. Of course, this will not satisfy those who read and believe what they learn in books like The Book of Urantia. For these folks, the Bible is merely a part of the whole, with Urantia going much further and a great deal deeper.

The trouble is that all of these books cannot be correct because there are problems when compared. Is the problem with the Bible, or with one of the other books? Of course, any problems I have seen so far are with these books, *not* the Bible. So in that sense, my viewpoint is slanted in favor of the validity of the Bible. That will certainly disappoint some who place their hopes, their life, and their faith in a work like *The Urantia Book*. Some will even pity me for what they perceive as my seeming closed-mindedness.

I'd also like to note that I have uncovered at least some contradictions in numerous works from this entire realm. Some have an explanation for that, though. More than one individual has said something similar to: "*Like most inspired works (the Bible for example), [Urantia] contains truth but is subject to interpretation and is not without error or distortion.*" That's one way to cover the bases, but it also assumes something else that may not be true. It assumes that the fault lies in the transference of the teaching to us, the students.

This fails to recognize that these beings – allegedly smarter, superior, and gifted way beyond us – are not able to transmit their thoughts, teachings, and tenets to us unfiltered. In other words, if they allegedly have flying machines that can zip from one end of the known universe (or beyond) to us and back in mere seconds or minutes, what is so difficult about sending us messages that we will understand without difficulty?

Why is it automatically assumed by some that within the realm of inter-dimensional or other worldly beings, they are incapable of presenting their thoughts to us in a way that allows them to be understood as they *wish* to be understood? Why are we giving them a pass on that one? It really makes little sense.

In fact, most people cast off the Bible for perceived contradictions. To them, these alleged nonconformities within the biblical record prove to them that the Bible cannot be trusted. However, when it comes to those messages received from those who claim to be higher beings, ascended masters, aliens, or what have you, it is accepted that these types of things are *"subject to interpretation and is not without error or distortion."*

This can only be due to the actual difference in *messages* between the Bible and all the rest. Whereas the Bible makes demands upon people in order to avoid eternal separation from God, messages and even dictated books alleged to be from entities beyond our sphere of living make no individual demands other than encouraging us to see our own good, and even our own godhood, in order that we might rise above it all and embrace our destiny. That destiny – as explained by these other beings – is to grant us passage to the next spiritual plane in our evolutionary journey.

What the Bible calls *evil*, books like *The Urantia Book* call misunderstanding. What the Scriptures refer to as eternal death, the musings of aliens simply call a mindset. The trouble with all of this is that once again, both cannot be correct. They can both be *wrong*, but they cannot both be correct because they are at odds with each other's teachings.

Throughout this book, I'm going to ask you repeatedly to look seriously at what you believe, and I am going to ask you to ask yourself *why* you believe as you do. Do you believe what you believe because it *feels* good and therefore addresses your inner conflict and sense of insecurity and inner conflict? Do you believe what you believe because it gives you the keys to your own success?

Ultimately, there is a reason you have chosen the path you are on and there is a reason you picked up this book. If you consider yourself to be a Christian, then I would ask you to verify that to yourself. Judge yourself based not on how you feel about yourself, but based on truth. That truth is found either in what you believe or it is not. It is not based on feelings, emotions, or even altruism. It is based on hard, cold facts.

NOISE FROM BEYOND

Before we get more deeply into analyzing *The Urantia Book*, let's take a bit of time to introduce and look briefly at several other works that have certainly had some impact on society if not the entire world. *A Course in Miracles, What is Scientology?,* and a book selected to be one out of many representative of that genre, *UFOs and the Extraterrestrial Message,* all offer insights into the mind and intellect of the entities that claim authorship of or at least are credited with sending important messages to earth.

Each of the aforementioned books enjoys a following of a specific type of person. As I've mentioned on numerous occasions previously, the people within the New Age are many and all come from varied backgrounds. What grabs the attention of one person may totally bore another.

This is what is so inviting about the New Age movement. There is not one overarching set of tenets that all must ascribe to in order to be part of the society. How much a person is involved in being part of the New Age movement is as varied as the individuals themselves.

While some believe in aliens from various planets within our universe, others find meaning from those they refer to as ascended masters. Still others find little that is personal within the New Age, preferring to see things as an impersonal force along the lines of George Lucas' *Star Wars* saga.

The New Age movement is all things to all people. No one thing is right for all people and not all things are right for all people. It is literally a smorgasbord of ideas, concepts, and beliefs. Because of this, it is not unusual that people who find the subject of aliens believable might never read *A Course in Miracles* or a book on the subject of *Scientology*. A person who sees validity in the Bible, yet rejects the seeming confines of Christianity, might gravitate toward *The Urantia Book*, because it offers *another* explanation for many of the Judeo-Christian concepts and doctrines that these folks have grown up understanding. In this way, directing their energies into reading and understanding what is taught in *The Urantia Book* allows them to continue to be believers in the Bible to some degree, but they wind up going *beyond* the orthodox view of Christianity as revealed in the Bible. These folks do not believe that they have left Christianity behind so much as they have simply moved *ahead* of the rest of us.

Do you see how within the New Age continuum, a person can rub elbows with someone with whom they would find little in common with, but they are both there because of their understanding of a *higher* view of life and the existence of humanity? The New Age movement provides in digestible bites what many believe Christianity does not.

A Course in Miracles

Helen Schucman is the name most synonymous with this work, which comprises several thousand pages. Originally published in three volumes in 1976 by the Foundation for Inner Peace, it has since undergone several new publications and can be obtained in one large volume.

This combined volume is broken down into a total of thirty-one chapters with numerous subtitles contained within each chapter. As you can see, topics range the religious and theological scale, responding to any number of questions – both asked and unasked – that the student may have regarding his or her life.

Chapter titles are as follows:

1. The Meaning of Miracles
2. The Separation and the Atonement
3. The Innocent Perception
4. The Illusions of the Ego
5. Healing and Wholeness
6. The Lessons of Love
7. The Gifts of the Kingdom
8. The Journey Back
9. The Acceptance of the Atonement
10. The Idols of Sickness
11. God or the Ego

12. The Holy Spirit's Curriculum
13. The Guiltless World
14. Teaching for Truth
15. The Holy Instant
16. The Forgiveness of Illusions
17. Forgiveness and the Holy Relationship
18. The Passing of the Dream
19. The attainment of Peace
20. The Vision of Holiness
21. Reason and Perception
22. Salvation and the Holy Relationship
23. The War Against Yourself
24. The Goal of Specialness
25. The Justice of God
26. The Transition
27. The Healing of the Dream
28. The Undoing of Fear
29. The Awakening
30. The New Beginning
31. The Final Vision

Other works have followed this one and serve mainly to clarify the original work, as well as to provide students with a workbook and give teachers a manual from which to teach.

The material that became *A Course in Miracles* is alleged to have been received by the Holy Spirit and given to Schucman. There is a great deal of religious and even biblical-sounding language throughout the work. That makes sense, because if the Holy Spirit (from the Judeo-Christian Bible) was the provider of the material, then it is clear that it would be thoroughly representative of what is taught in the Bible.

If this is not the case – that the authentic Holy Spirit provided the material – then it is equally clear that an imposter provided the material to Schucman. In doing so, it is understandable then why this impost-

Why Should We Believe Them?

er Holy Spirit would couch much of its teachings in language reminiscent of Christianity and the Bible. Doing so would produce the desired effect of bringing people into the circle by letting down their defenses. They would meet terms and phrases of which they were familiar and because of that would easily be drawn into the scenario presented by Schucman's Holy Spirit.

We will spend some time highlighting some of the teaching in *Miracles*, and it will be compared with the teaching of the Bible and specifically with the words of Jesus.

What is Scientology?

While not a book written *by* L. Ron Hubbard, it is understood to be a work *based* on Hubbard's own work. Moreover, this book was *compiled* by the organization that Hubbard founded: The Church of Scientology International. What better organization would there be to gather the writings and teachings of their founder than the administration of Scientology itself?

The book – composed of over 750 pages – deals with any number of areas that are important to the mental health and well-being of people everywhere. For instance, the contents of the book tell us what is meant by the *State of Clear, What Total Freedom Means, Why Scientologists Believe They Have Lived Before, What the E-Meter is and How it Works, Why Scientology is a Religion for People of All Religions, How Scientology Began*, and more. Here is the listing of the forty-one chapters:

1. The Scientology Religion
2. The Religious Heritage of Scientology
3. L. Ron Hubbard, the Founder of Scientology

4. A Description of Scientology
5. The Practice of Scientology
6. The Bridge to a Better Life
7. Basic Dianetics and Scientology
8. Dianetics and Scientology Introductory Services
9. Revitalizing the Individual in a Polluted and Drugged World
10. Study Technology: Effective Learning and Education
11. The Key to Life: Handling a World Out of Communication
12. The Life Orientation Course: Attaining Competence in Life
13. The Grade Chart: Auditing to Higher States of Existence
14. The Classification Chart: Auditor Training Services
15. Recommended Course of Progress
16. Chaplain and Ministerial Services
17. Scientology Ethics and Judicial Matters
18. Any Reasons for Difficulties and Their Correction
19. Successes of Scientology
20. Structure of Scientology Churches
21. Churches, Missions, and Groups
22. The Management of Scientology
23. The Guarnator of Scientology's Future
24. The International Association of Scientologists
25. The Staff of Scientology Churches
26. The Church of Scientology
27. Scientology Volunteer Ministers
28. Spearheading Social Reform
29. WISE: Enabling Groups to Flourish and Prosper
30. Solutions to a Troubled Society
31. Demographic and Statistical Facts About Scientology
32. The History of Scientology's Expansion
33. Future Prediction of Scientology
34. Those Who Oppose Scientology
35. Answers to Common Questions
36. The Bona Fides of the Scientology Religion

37. L. Ron Hubbard: A Chronicle
38. L. Ron Hubbard: How His Work Has Influenced the World
39. The Creeds and Codes of Scientology
40. The Axioms of Dianetics and Scientology
41. List of Churches of Scientology and Other Related Organizations

The important part of Scientology is what it teaches, not who is allegedly attacking it, or why it has been audited. That part has more to do with L. Ron Hubbard than anything else. In essence, a system is known by what it teaches, and because of that, it is very important to understand exactly what those tenets and precepts are so that truth can be discerned.

Is Scientology that far off from *A Course in Miracles*? We'll see if we can determine that.

UFOs and the Extraterrestrial Message
This book claims to be *"a spiritual insight into UFOs and cosmic transmissions."* Of course, what is interesting here is that right from the starting blocks, we understand that the author of this work, Richard Lawrence (not to be confused with Christian author Richard O. Lawrence), is presenting a message to his readers that asks and even expects them to take his book as truth, and that truth is connected with extraterrestrial beings.

This book is 186 pages in length; a fairly quick read. It contains nine chapters labeled as follows:

1. The Arrival of Flying Saucers
2. They Make Contact

Why Should We Believe Them?

3. X-Files, Cover-ups, and Downright Lies
4. A Close Encounter in Hampshire
5. ETs in Ancient Records and Religions
6. Life in a Multidimensional Universe
7. Mysticism and the Masters
8. Primary Terrestrial Mental Channel
9. The Extraterrestrial Message

As we'll see, throughout Lawrence's book one message and testimony after another regarding the teachings of aliens is presented. The book does not attempt to prove anything it puts forth. It simply expects the text to speak for itself and have the desired impact on the reader. That impact is for the reader to believe that this universe contains many entities not part of the earth system. Though not part of it, they are indirectly related to it and seek to break through to us in order to help better our own environs.

There are literally a plethora of these types of books available to the public, and interest in aliens, extraterrestrials, and dimensional beings has long been a fascination of society. Within the past few decades, this area has come under greater scrutiny even among Christians.

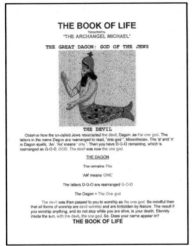

The Book of Life
This book was purportedly transcribed by *the* Archangel Michael of the Bible fame. You know, he's the angel who is the protector of Israel, at least according to Scripture. He introduces himself in this book by presenting his credentials from the Bible, quoting numerous places from Matthew to Revelation, and even referring to Genesis.

Once having explained who he is and

why he has taken the time to write the material he wrote, he then spends the remainder of the book explaining the *real* truth regarding God, the Bible, Adam and Eve, sin, Jesus, and all the rest.

This is allegedly the case of an archangel supposedly given permission to honestly explain things where the Bible has apparently not been clear, or where people have allegedly confused the issue through misinterpretation or simply bad translations.

In one sense, all of these books have the same thing in common. Either directly or indirectly, they purport to have a connection with beings beyond our realm. Whether they are ascended masters or extraterrestrials is not the point because those are simply names we have given them, or in some cases, they have given themselves. The authentic point is that our world is connected to their realms via their voices and their thoughts. It is allegedly through their desire to teach us that we even know about them in the first place. It is their purported concern for us and this earth that many of them say they had a hand in creating that caused them to breach the gap between our dimension and theirs.

These beings tell us they are *there*, just outside of our physical realm, but *within* our spiritual realm, to help us and bring us to their level of existence. It will come – they say – through a submission to their ideals and an acceptance of their goals.

This is what they present to us and they cannot overemphasize the need to ignore any concerns we may have and embrace their message fully. Doing so will save us. Ignoring them will reap total destruction.

Will it? Yes and no...

THE NEW AGE

This is probably a good time to briefly explain what the New Age is all about and why it is important to understand it, especially in this current time in which we live. At its most basic, the New Age is a system of beliefs that are alleged to bring each person to the next spiritual plane of existence. This is done through literally putting off the old, worn out, out-of-date religious systems to which people have aligned themselves for centuries and literally getting back to nature.

Why Should We Believe Them?

The basic tenets of New Age thought are comprised of several areas that help people do this, it is said. The more people become experienced practitioners of New Age thought and practice, the more adept they become at unlocking their own inner divinity and growing beyond themselves.

Constance E. Cumby has written several books on the subject, and I refer to her because in many ways she was the first on the scene to point out the problems with the New Age movement years ago. To many the New Age might not seem to be problematic, and that's usually because those people are simply seeing the very tip of the pyramid, so to speak.

These people see just what's on or just under the surface, but they do not see the base of the pyramid, or the foundation of that pyramid. The movers and shakers who have literally partnered to create the New Age system (which in nearly all respects, dates back to Nimrod in Genesis 11 and the Tower of Babel) have done so well at covering the base and foundation that in large measure, it is so well hidden from the average individual that they would never find out what it entails…unless it is pointed out to them.

In one very real sense, the New Age movement is the largest cult in the world – and it is one that has existed the longest, having altered its form as needed to entrap and keep entrapped as many people as possible over the centuries of time that humanity has existed. If we consider what makes a cult, it is generally a religious system that contains some type of secret (or new) knowledge (gnosis). This knowledge is not necessarily available to new adherents. In order to learn about this knowledge, one must prove themselves to be loyal. As one remains with the system over time, new things are learned, and then eventually, when loyalty is proven, the deeper secrets are revealed. This is why it takes more than *one* cult to trap people, because what works for one will not work for another.

Why Should We Believe Them?

This is exactly how cults work. All the deep, dark secrets are hidden way beneath the surface. Only those who follow all the rules and prove their loyalty beyond question are allowed into that "winner's" circle.

But let's take a moment or two to find out what the New Age really wants to achieve. Are they as altruistic as they pretend to be, or is there something far more malevolent going on behind the scenes?

Ultimately, the New Age movement truly has its modern origin with Madame Blavatsky, who was at the forefront of the Theosophical Society, which is essentially an esoteric society of occultism. Alice A. Bailey picked up the ball after Blavatsky's death. Both of these women wrote prolific works, generally attributed to their own personal guide, or ascended master.

Most believe that the tenets of the New Age are nothing more than ideals that all human beings should seek to achieve. If we do, we will then simply become a better society, as we will learn to overcome war and peace will be the normal practice of the day. This is the New Age that most people are aware of and to them it seems very altruistic and certainly not malevolent.

An excellent book on the subject of the New Age – its origin, meaning, and goals – can be found in Constance Cumbey's book *The Hidden Dangers of the Rainbow*. Cumbey has received a great deal of criticism and even hostility due to her teaching on the New Age, including the fact that she has named specific organizations and names that are big players in the New Age movement.

The contents of Cumbey's book are as follows:
- *Maitreya: The New Age Messiah*
- *Awakening to the New Age Movement*
- *The Age of Aquarius? Or the Age of the Antichrist?*
- *The Movement: A Short History*

- *The Movement: An Overview*
- *The New Age and Prophecy*
- *Structure and Front Organizations*
- *The New Age Movement – the Fourth Reich?*
- *Infiltration, Recruitment and Conditioning*
- *A New Age of Satanism?*
- *Deluded…or Deceivers?*
- *The Old Lie: Finding God Within*
- *How to Help New Agers*
- *Appendix A: Selected New Age Organizations*
- *Appendix B: The 'Great Invocation' Distribution*
- *Appendix C: The Unity-in-Diversity Council*
- *Appendix D: A Message from Benjamin Crème*
- *Appendix E: The New Group of World Servers*
- *Appendix F: Lucis Trust – World Goodwill Newsletter*
- *Appendix G: The Hidden Dangers of the Rainbow*
- *Selected Bibliography*

Cumbey wrote the book in 1983 and I cannot recommend it enough. It is a book that needs to be read and studied, and in many ways, it was written ahead of its time. It seems to be much more contemporary now, even though it was very important when it was first written years ago.

The reality of the New Age is far more than simply a very loose knit organization of people who simply want peace at all costs and believe it can be achieved through a mindset, meditation, and visualization. It goes well beyond this to the actual dangers that are present within the network that makes up the New Age. Tragically, the average practitioner of a New Age program goes through life completely unaware of the movers and shakers within the movement itself. Again, I would invite the reader to avail themselves of Cumbey's previously mentioned book because she details aspects of the New Age movement of which most are simply unaware.

Cumbey explains that too many people – often poor and underprivileged – have become involved in aspects of the New Age movement through what she calls *front organizations*. These people got involved because they "*had a sincere and genuine concern for the world's poor and labored under the mistaken impression that they were lending their support to a remedy for the world's numerous wrongs. They were unsuspecting that they were supporting a movement that parallels Naziism in every grotesque detail, including a teaching that a 'blood taint' rested on those of Jewish extraction and another being that of a planned new 'super race'.*"[4]

This is the biggest tragedy of the New Age movement. It is *not* what it seems. In some ways, it is the largest cult in existence, bar none. The reason for that is due to the fact that the New Age teachings can and have affected nearly every area of society: television, music, books, movies, and even over the past several decades, within *churches*.

Essentially, the coming new world order that many speak of today ties in nicely with the New Age movement. Ideologically, in order to become part of the coming new world order, a Luciferic initiation must be experienced by each person. Again, most do not know of this, and when it does happen it will seem natural, simply part of the continuing and growing process of societal expansion.

At its very base, the New Age movement deifies Satan, or Lucifer as they prefer to call him. They believe that through their efforts, Lucifer will one day reign supreme, and his loyal followers with him. Of course, this may sound very far-fetched to the average individual;

---

[4] Constance Cumbey, *The Hidden Dangers of the Rainbow* (Huntington House 1993), 16

and that is exactly the way the leaders within the New Age movement prefer it, because it sounds so preposterous it is difficult for the average person to believe and accept. This very fact also naturally puts these people at odds with those who try to teach the truth about the New Age.

The Luciferic initiation ultimately leads the adherent to submit to Satan himself. It begins through a spiritual initiation or phase that has already been in the works. This has been going on throughout various outlets like Hollywood, music, TV, books, and more for generations. It has slowly been creating a resistance within people to the orthodoxy of Christianity, while at the same time has opened their minds to the potential of New Age thought, of which the kernel is "ye shall be as gods."

"Options in the Plan: Initiation or Death/Initiation and Death[.] All who wish to enter the New Age must undergo an 'energy activation' or 'rebirth', usually marked by a subjective trance-induced 'light experience' where one meets either a 'spirit guide' or one's 'higher self' (no difference since all is one). The resulting 'altered state of consciousness' will eventually lead to a 'Luciferic initiation' into the 'new humanity', or a submission to Lucifer as the leading divinity representing the Logos."[5]

Luciferic initiation *opens* the door to Satan and invites him in through the giving up of the person's will. In other words, people will turn their minds and volition over to Satan without realizing it because the experience they will undergo will be pleasant by all standards. This experience predicated on an altered state opens the mind to the demonic realm. Once that door opens, he wastes no time in stepping

---

[5] http://www.cephasministry.com/new_age_initiation.html

through it. The more people he can control or influence, the greater his power on earth will become.

But what is most interesting is that the New Age can simply be a mantra or a phrase included within popular music that at first gains someone's attention, then enraptures them through it. In the 1980s a type of music called *Black Metal* began in Oslo, Norway. It was unique, new, and in every respect completely *mystifying*...for certain types of people. It is a *"loose term used to describe a handful of extreme metal bands who shared traits such as 'shrieked' vocals, high-pitched guitar tones, raw recording, and 'Satanic' lyrics."*[6] As can be imagined, it contained a strong anti-Christian flavor and sentiment. This led to actual church burnings. As can be imagined, the content of this style of music is controversial at best and satanic at worst.

One of the major acts of that period was Varg Vikernes, whose *Burzum* project created a huge cult following. Interestingly enough, Vikernes was eventually found guilty of murdering a guitarist from another group and also of torching several churches.

The New Age literally has something for everyone, and we have spent time cataloguing this fact in previous books. This is what is so intriguing for most about the New Age because it is not simply contained in one thing. Whether it's a form of "church," music, movies, mantras, meditation, or something else entirely, it is literally able to fit into just about any mold.

Recently, a movie called "Tree of Life" won top honors at Cannes. The movie *"stars Brad Pitt, Sean Penn and Jessica Chastain in a far-flung story of family life that plays out against a cosmic backdrop, in-*

---

[6] http://en.wikipedia.org/wiki/Early_Norwegian_black_metal_scene (5/21/11)

cluding glorious visuals of the creation of the universe and the era of dinosaurs."[7]

It is a movie that emphasizes the good in people, and says the way to better a person's life is through training to be more selfless. This is one of the seemingly altruistic tenets within the New Age. Less of self is better.

That is absolutely true, but the problem is that the Bible teaches throughout that trying to become selfless through our own energy and strength does not amount to much as far as God is concerned. To other people, it may seem that we are truly bettering ourselves, but to God it means nothing. His Word says, *"But we are all as an unclean thing, and all our righteousnesses are as filthy rags; and we all do fade as a leaf; and our iniquities, like the wind, have taken us away. And there is none that calleth upon thy name, that stirreth up himself to take hold of thee: for thou hast hid thy face from us, and hast consumed us, because of our iniquities"* (Isaiah 64:6-7). The truth of the matter is we are affected and infected by and with sin. Because of that, anything we might do in our own strength to improve our situation fails miserably from God's perspective.

That's like changing a dirty band-aid to a new, clean one. The problem is that it covers the same wound. We can dress ourselves up on the outside, but inside we are as filthy rags, and it simply only *appears* outwardly that we are good or improving. God looks at our life and compares it to only one Person: Jesus. We, on the other hand, constantly compare our lives with other people, and it is easy to find something that we believe is far worse off than we are now. While that is true – outwardly – the reality is that sin has still affected all

---

[7] http://movies.msn.com/movies/article.aspx?news=648805&gt1=28101 (5/22/11)

people, and because of that, we need something radical to occur in our life.

Jesus explained this clearly in John 3 to Nicodemus when He told him that it would take being born again, or being born from above. This is the only way that a new life would occur, canceling out our sin and ultimately redeeming us from our sinful nature.

But people do not want to hear this because the sin nature, along with the enemy of our souls, has worked it so that we are automatically antagonistic to God, even though He offers us eternal life.

We try everything else in a vain attempt to gain what can only be gained through faith in Jesus' life, death, and resurrection. We try meditation, 12 Steps, promises, resolution, and we try in our own strength, but it does not fly with God.

Movies like "The Tree of Life" emphasize man's ability to perfect himself, or at least place himself on that path that leads to betterment. The extended synopsis, as listed on IMDB.com, states, *"Tree of Life is a period film centered around three boys in the 1950s. The eldest son of two characters (Brad Pitt and Jessica Chastain) witnesses the loss of innocence.*

"We trace the evolution of Jack, an eleven-year-old boy in the Midwest, who is one of three brothers. At first, the world seems marvelous to the child. He sees everything as his mother does, with the eyes of his soul. She represents the way of love and mercy, while the father tries to teach his son the world's way, of putting oneself first. Each parent tries to influence Jack, who must reconcile their claims with each other. The picture darkens as he has his first glimpses of sickness, suffering and death. The world, once a thing of glory, becomes a labyrinth.

"Framing this story is the life of adult Jack (Sean Penn); a lost soul in a modern world, seeking to discover amid the changing scenes of time that which does not change: the eternal scheme of which we are a part.

When he sees all that has gone into our world's preparation, each thing appears a miracle precious and incomparable. Jack, with his new understanding, is able to forgive his father and take his first steps on the path of life. From this story is that of adult Jack, a lost soul in a modern world.

"The story ends in hope, acknowledging the beauty and joy in all things, in the everyday and above all in the family -- our first school -- the only place that most of us learn the truth about the world and ourselves, or discover life's single most important lesson, of unselfish love."[8]

The movie "The Tree of Life" will open to rousing cheers of self-effort and the ability to learn to love one another and just get along by becoming selfless. In many ways, of course, this has a note of religion to it, doesn't it, but without all the trappings of religion. There's no book, there's no one God, there are simply tenets and thoughts. It's as easy as that. This is what makes the New Age the most dangerous thing on the planet. It has this innate ability to morph into something that hits the needs of every single person alive.

As far as the recognized (though often deeply hidden) leaders of the New Age are concerned, they have determined that entering the new world order will only occur through the Luciferic initiation, and those who refuse will be eliminated. It's really that simple, and because of its nature, it is kept hidden. However, at the same time, would the average person believe this was the deep, dark motivation of the New Age? The world will arrive to the point where those who refuse to unite themselves with the rest of the world will of necessity need to be exterminated. There will be no room for alternate or opposing ideologies in the coming new world order.

---

[8] http://www.imdb.com/title/tt0478304/synopsis (accessed 5/22/11)

How often is this fact brought out? How often do you hear people talking openly about an alleged Luciferic initiation? It's rare, and certainly it is not discussed openly. Most are simply unaware of it and are content to have no knowledge of it, because they believe that their own peculiar philosophies that have placed them squarely within the New Age are just that, *philosophies* that allow them to gain a better perspective on life itself. Because of that, they also think that through this set of beliefs that have become their own philosophical viewpoint, they will be able to aspire to be something far greater than they are today. It moves them toward the goal of perfection, or at least a greater sense of goodness than they have previously thought possible.

The image above is becoming far more obvious in today's society. *Behind* this image is the concept that all people *should* be able to simply get along irrespective of the differences between one person's beliefs and another's. However, if we simply consider the fact that Christianity is opposed to Islam as well as some of the other religions represented by their logos, and Islam is opposed to everything else, there is no way that all of these various ideologies can come to a point of true co-existence *unless* all within each of those groups give up some of the major beliefs that make them unique.

In essence, it is actually *impossible* for various religions to learn to co-exist (interdependently on one another) and still remain uniquely independent of the other. This is due to the fact that there are way too many unique beliefs that separate one group from another.

For instance, Christianity by its very nature believes that the only way to God is through Jesus. Islam believes that Muhammad is the true prophet through whom all people must go to gain any form of salvation. Other groups are less dogmatic and can incorporate aspects of other religions and ideologies without too much difficulty and without cutting their nose off to spite their face.

For a Christian to do this, they cease to take seriously their commitment to Jesus. Islam is the same way, with those who would compromise betraying their loyalty to Allah. The naiveté of people who believe that all that needs to happen for peace to occur is that people learn to co-exist regardless of ideology reveals a desire for a new world order predicated on the tenets taught within the New Age movement.

As far as the New Age is concerned, many are looking forward to the coming of a man of peace, who will actually usher in peace, especially in the Middle East. This man is known as Maitreya, and his identity has not been directly revealed yet because he himself remains in the shadows. However, people like Benjamin Crème believe that Maitreya has been revealed to him. Others believe this as well.

Maitreya is understood to be the messiah that will bring in the New Age. Benjamin Crème has been talking about Maitreya for decades. He is being sought, and his desired appearing is rapidly becoming the talk at coffee bars and restaurants.

According to Cumbey, Maitreya is believed to "*be the fifth reincarnation of Buddha. The world's Buddhists are already expecting Lord Maitreya to return to earth. So, the name was a very shrewd choice.*

"*In order to appeal to Christians, New Agers say Maitreye is the Christ. For Moslems he is the Imam Mahdi. For Hindus he is Krishna.*

"*Maitreya's followers are now in the last state of the New Age scheme to take the world for Lucifer.*

"Lucis Trust – formerly Lucifer Trust – ran ads in the Reader's Digest, *which displayed The Great Invocation to Maitreya.*

"The Great Invocation refers to The Plan. It says, 'Let Light and Love and Power restore The Plan on earth'."[9]

I have talked about The Plan on my radio show, and in essence, bringing The Plan to fruition means to usher in the new – and final – world order. This particular order will also see the rise of the New Age "messiah" in the form of Maitreya.

According to Benjamin Crème, Maitreya has been living on the earth since July of 1977. Apparently, Maitreya was supposed to reveal himself to the world, but things have not gone as planned and he has yet to do so. A few years ago, without directly saying it, Benjamin Crème *implied* that the Maitreya was indeed Raj Patel. Patel is known for his book *The Value of Nothing*.

What is fascinating about Patel, aside from the question of whether or not he is in fact Maitreya, as Crème suggests (and to my knowledge, Patel has never denied or agreed with this), is his blink rate. It is almost as if he does not need to blink. That may seem extremely minor or even nothing at all, but there is something strange about that.

Patel was born in 1972. He is a *"British-born American academic, journalist, activist and writer who has lived and worked in Zimbabwe, South Africa and the United States for extended periods. He is best known for his 2008 book, Stuffed and Starved: The Hidden Battle for the World Food System. His most recent book is The Value of Nothing which was on The New York Times best-seller list during February*

---

[9] Constance Cumbey, *The Hidden Dangers of the Rainbow* (Huntington House 1993), 20-21

2010. He has been referred to as "the rock star of social justice writing."[10]

So *is* Patel Maitreya? I have no idea, and only time will tell. I'm certainly not suggesting that, but it is clear that whoever the person is who turns out to be the Maitreya is also clearly the Antichrist.

Patel is an interesting person, but we need to wait until the final revelation. I only include his name here because of his indirect association to Benjamin Crème.

I suppose a good question to at least wonder about is why Maitreya has not revealed himself officially to the world yet. What's keeping him from doing so?

If you ask leaders within the New Age, the answer is along the lines of what you would expect. Maitreya cannot reveal himself to the world yet because forces have been working to keep him hidden. These forces are considered to be malevolent and are working to keep the coming "good" from occurring. Of course, it probably does not need to be clarified that these malevolent forces are none other than Bible-believing Christians.

That is the thing with Satan. He likely knows far more about God's plan than the most faithful and loyal authentic Christian. However, Satan does not know every aspect of God's plan, and he certainly does not know the timing of things in most cases.

This is at least one reason he has been busy telling practitioners of the New Age about the coming reveal of Maitreya, as well as the coming "Great Evacuation" that will essentially remove 20 million or more people from the face of the earth in an instant. Sounds like the Rapture to me.

---

[10] http://en.wikipedia.org/wiki/Raj_Patel (accessed 5/21/11)

Satan knows these things *will* occur, but he does not know *when* they will occur. So he keeps pushing himself on society through a variety of avenues in preparation for that day when he – through Antichrist – will walk onto the world's stage and begin the process of creating an empire in which he becomes the absolute dictator. This is chilling in all respects, but the truth is that Satan can only do what God allows, and he can only do it when God allows. It is ultimately God's timetable, not Satan's.

The Bible tells us that *"the mystery of iniquity doth already work: only he who now letteth will let, until he be taken out of the way.*

"And then shall that Wicked be revealed, whom the Lord shall consume with the spirit of his mouth, and shall destroy with the brightness of his coming:

"Even him, whose coming is after the working of Satan with all power and signs and lying wonders,

"And with all deceivableness of unrighteousness in them that perish; because they received not the love of the truth, that they might be saved" (2 Thessalonians 2:7-10).

If you look at the first verse, we learn that even though iniquity (evil) is already well established in society and continuing its pressure to grow throughout society more than it is now, there is something that holds it back. Whatever is holding this evil back will do so until "he" is no longer there to restrain the evil.

The evil Paul is referring to here is ultimately the Antichrist (man of sin). In spite of what he would like to do, he cannot reveal himself to the world until he is allowed to so. That will come when "he" is taken out of the way. Of course, theologians have disagreed over the identity of "he" here, but I believe that the Bible is referring to the Holy Spirit as He works through the authentic Church.

Once the Church is removed during the Rapture, consider the fact that a tremendous dam *against* evil will no longer be here. This does not mean that the Holy Spirit leaves the earth. It simply means that one of His main vehicles to introduce people to Jesus as Savior and Lord is now gone. With this absence, the ultimate and final evil in the form of Antichrist will be allowed onto the world's stage.

The New Age can only do so much to gain converts and to infiltrate society as a whole. Once the Church is gone, the largest restraining power of the Holy Spirit against evil and all that is not God will also be moved aside. In will flow evil in immeasurable volumes.

You won't hear the New Age leaders tell us this, though, because they are simply unaware of it. They believe that timing is everything, and the reveal of Maitreya awaits a time when more people will believe in him and receive them into their hearts. It is the first phase of the Luciferic initiation, as we have discussed.

I have watched a number of videos on the Internet where Benjamin Crème has been "overshadowed" by Maitreya. In most cases, Crème allows Maitreya to speak through him. However, in at least one video, it was clear that Maitreya's voice came out of thin air. Crème's lips never moved and he simply gazed at the audience.

The voice of Maitreya through Crème is recognizably British because Crème himself is from Great Britain and has that accent. However, in this one video where Crème seemed to speak apart from Crème, the accent was gone. In fact, Maitreya's voice sounded like something out of a Sci-Fi movie from decades ago; except, of course, it had a message from today. The message was simply along the lines of Maitreya asking adherents to allow him to work in and through them so that he might expand his kingdom.

As we have stated before, Satan needs permission of individuals to come into their lives and take over. He needed this with Adam and

Eve and he needs it today. When Adam and Eve succumbed to his temptations and ate of the fruit of the tree, they literally turned the title deed of the earth over to Satan. This is exactly why Jesus refers to Satan as having a kingdom – a kingdom of darkness. Paul says that Satan is the prince of the power of the air (cf. Ephesians 2:1-2). Satan offered all the kingdoms of this world to Jesus when he tempted Jesus in the wilderness (Matthew 4). Jesus never disputed the claim, though He did successfully avoid the temptations.

In spite of the fact that Satan has title deed to the earth, he still needs an invite to get into people's heads and control their wills. Drugs can do that. Ouija boards can do it. Tarot cards can do it. Anything that is within the realm of the things that God has forbidden (cf. Deuteronomy 18) opens the door to Satan. Once Satan gains access, he fights to keep control.

What people do not realize about the New Age movement is that it is headed up by *someone*. It did not simply originate in a vacuum and carry itself along from generation to generation on the wings of the wind. Though it may appear to the average individual as something quite harmless and unincorporated, it is quite the opposite.

Satan is obviously the ultimate creator of the New Age movement that actually began in Genesis 11 and the Tower of Babel. There, Nimrod tried to unite the people as one, teaching them that they could do anything they set their minds to doing. God intervened and dispersed people through the use of various languages and cultures.

The New Age at its root is nothing more than "ye shall be as gods." This lie, which Satan used to tempt Eve in the Garden of Eden (Genesis 2-3) and that resulted in the fall of humanity, has been the hallmark of the New Age movement since.

Satan has been working through humanity to gain the upper hand, just as he gained the upper hand in Eden, and as he nearly gained the upper hand at the Tower of Babel. Satan has worked and had his work cut off or stopped by God. Satan has not given up, however, and each time God has stopped him, he has come back with more vehemence.

This of course does not mean that Satan will eventually succeed, though it will certainly appear to be the case for a short period of time. What it means is that God simply kept Satan at bay until the proper time when all things will be fulfilled. That time is coming and in fact is now here. What I mean by that is that the overall period of time is here now, and has been for a while.

As I write this, it is eleven minutes after Midnight, and Sunday morning, May 22, 2011 has just begun on the West Coast. A guy by the name of Harold Camping predicted the world was going to end...*yesterday*. It didn't, and I'm still writing this.

I am not talking about that type of stupidity. I am referring to the fact that the Bible teaches us that an end or last age is coming, and it is my studied opinion that humanity is now living in that time. How long will this time period last before the last seven years take place? I have no idea, but I do know that based on the Bible, when those final seven years occur – The Tribulation – it will usher in the period when the Antichrist steps up to the plate and eventually gains worldwide worship as Maitreya, Mahdi, and even The Christ. Unfortunately, he will most certainly not be Christ.

Ever since the Garden of Eden, Satan has desired to be worshiped by all. He has never given up this dream, and it is for this dream he works tirelessly. God will allow Satan to have his day, and he will experience it through Antichrist himself. God will allow this in order for His own specific purposes to be fulfilled.

The New Age movement appears very loose knit, and in a very real sense does not even seem as though there is a guiding force behind it.

Why Should We Believe Them?

This is the malevolent beauty of it, because though it appears to be simply something that is carried along on the ideas of people wishing nothing but goodwill to one another, it is far more insidious and dangerous than that.

The Luciferic initiation that I spoke of previously is the capstone of all that the New Age is working toward. It will culminate in the taking of a mark by each individual. Those who refuse the mark will, of course, not fulfill the initiation requirements.

This mark, whatever it is – something the Bible says equals the number of man (666) – will forever separate the sheep from the goats, literally. Those who take the mark will find themselves separated from God for all eternity because they will in fact have committed themselves to the worship of Lucifer.

Lucifer – as far as the New Age is concerned – is the Solar God and Solar Logos. This being is already being served and worshiped by those far up in the New Age movement. They see Lucifer (not Satan) as the one, true god. He got a raw deal from Jesus, and because of that has been forever attempting to regain what was taken from him.

New Age guru David Spangler has stated, *"Christ is the same force as Lucifer...Lucifer prepares man for the experience of Christhood. [He is] the great initiator...Lucifer works with each of us to bring us to wholeness and as we move into a New Age...each of us in some way is brought to that point which I term the Luciferic Initiation...for it is an invitation into the New Age."*[11]

Others who helped catapult the New Age movement into the mainstream have stated as much as well. Alice A. Bailey refers to Lucifer

---

[11] David Spangler *Reflections on the Christ* (1978), 44-45

as *"the Lord of the world"*[12] and Joseph Carr has told us that Lucifer *"is releasing new energies into the world to bring for the much-need 'principle of sharing'."*[13]

The second phase of the Luciferic initiation is physical, as mentioned. It is receiving the mark that permanently and eternally identifies each adherent with Lucifer. The Bible tells us that this mark will be either on the right hand or the forehead (cf. Revelation 13:16; 14:11). According to the Bible, those who take the mark are doomed forever.

The New Age seems sublime, healthy, and innocuous. It is far from it, and though we can take no more time to discuss it, I would encourage everyone reading this to do their own research. Get Constance Cumbey's book. It is well worth having.

In many ways, the world is on the cusp of this burgeoning New Age. One man will rise above all and though his appearance will seem loving, inviting, soothing, and even accepting of all people, he will eventually turn against the entire world, demanding absolute worship. He will be the final dictator that Satan will personally create and embody.

Those within the New Age who are well known to us through their books and lectures – Benjamin Crème, Marilyn Ferguson, David Spangler and many others – have been teaching of the coming world messiah for decades. They have spent their life opening up a world to the coming Age of Aquarius, which they promise will be the beginning of eternal peace on earth, where no one will go hungry, no one will ever be in harm's way, and all will live in absolute and unending peace. The problem, though, is that it comes with a price, and the price is very high. It is your soul. Your soul in exchange for all these

---

[12] Joseph Carr *The Lucifer Connection,* 140
[13] Alice A. Bailey *The Destiny of the Nations*

things. Are you willing to risk that? Is your soul worth so little that you would trade it to Satan for the false promises that he will be unable to deliver?

I pray not...

DECISIONS, DECISIONS

Most people believe that they have little to no problem discerning the truth. Most people are wrong. The plain fact of the matter is that there are too many debates about things that are supposedly truth that often leave people with no clear understanding of just exactly what truth is and how it looks.

If you have ever taken the time to enter any informal debate, it is clear that there are often no real winners, and rarely does anyone change his or her mind following the discussion. The topic might center on a sports team, or some political candidate, or religion, and the only thing that is actually clear when all is said and done is that people have *opinions* and they know how to state – at times rather vociferously – those opinions.

It really doesn't matter how firm someone is or even how convinced they are of the truthfulness of their own position. Convincing others of the alleged truth of that position is often easier said than done.

Take the time to listen to any of the political pundits on television and you know what I mean. In fact, there are pundits for every area of interest, whether it's food, sports, religion, politics, cars, exercise, and more. The list is endless and within each area, people are ready and willing to debate based on how they view things.

Having said all that, as noted in the beginning of this book, there of necessity *must* be one truth. There has to be something that is beyond humanity's opinion that stands for all time and eternity as *the* truth. If there isn't, then no one does anything wrong. If there is not one all-encompassing truth, then laws are pointless because they are simply based on humanity's *opinion* of what is right and wrong. If there is no truth to back those laws up, then they remain merely opinions.

Certainly, some people (including some judges) treat laws as if they *are* merely opinions. These type of people willingly set laws aside on a whim because it does not suit their lifestyle. People who do this are normally referred to as *criminals*. Judges who do this are normally referred to as *activists*.

Would you agree with me that there must be *one* truth that supersedes everything? If there is not, then you are wasting your time reading this book, as I have wasted my time in writing it.

If you will agree with me that there is one overarching truth that not only supersedes everything, but on that basis is the one thing that is constant, then all that is left is determining what that specific truth is all about and how it affects us and the world.

It is clear that I believe the Bible to be that truth because it represents God's Word to humanity. Not all truth is contained in the Bible, but all that is contained in the Bible is truth.

You may believe that *A Course in Miracles* is *the* truth. Someone else may believe that *The Urantia Book* contains the actual truth. What we are left with, then, is trying to find a way to convince one another that the truth each of us holds as true is the only truth that is available and everything else is a lie.

As noted, that is difficult if not impossible to do, because ultimately the decision regarding anyone else's "truth" is at the mercy of the individual who will decide whose truth is the correct truth. The only way I can see to do that is by going through highlights of each of the books previously mentioned and comparing them with the Bible. Doing so may still not convince you or anyone else that it is the Bible that contains absolute truth. Again, that is for you to decide. I cannot, nor would not, deign to force you to accept my understanding of truth as contained within the Bible. The only thing I can do is make a good case for it, and that is certainly what I am going to try to do.

Let's start with *The Urantia Book* to determine what it says about the life of Jesus on earth. As previously noted, it is very in-depth, with much to claim about Jesus. The obvious thing to do is to take what is stated and compare it with Scripture. There *will* be variances and even contradictions between the two records. Your responsibility is to determine for yourself what you believe to be the truth and *why* you believe it to be that truth. Failing here means you are believing a guess at best and a lie at worst.

It's probably fair to say that most of us make decisions based on *consequences*. We weigh what we consider to be evidence and then based on that evidence, we move to one way or another. For instance, a decision about which college to attend can be time-consuming. It involves a great many things, like overall costs, distance from home, degree options and more. In order to make a decision here, all things need to be considered. Ultimately, the *consequences* of attending a particular college or university are also part of the equation. Will a person have more job and career opportunities with one college over another?

Buying a home or a car, accepting a job offer, marrying someone, deciding to have children – all of these decisions and more are arrived at through a careful consideration of all that is involved, including the consequences of each decision. Most would agree that these types of decisions fall into the amoral decision arena. The moral compass that each person holds within them is not necessarily part of the process in making these types of decisions, but at the same time, *could* be part of the process.

When it comes to moral areas, often it appears as though the decisions we make there do not involve the same type of mental gymnastics. We often make a decision based on how we *feel* about something, and sometimes we make a decision based on the spur of the moment.

Recently, the public learned that a well-known personality was found to have cheated on his wife. He apparently literally got in bed with a member of the household staff a decade and a half ago and fathered a child. He did this while married to his current wife who, upon hearing this news, promptly moved out.

This type of decision that the man made – to commit adultery – was likely based on something that spurred him to act on his *impulses*. In this case, he did not stop to consider anything, much less the *consequences* of such a decision. He may have toyed with the idea in his head for some time with the obligatory flirting that may have gone on between the two; or, in the heat of the moment, he may have simply sensed that there was a chemical attraction and, as they say, *went for it*. Had he stopped to consider the ramifications of his actions, that may have been enough to stop him from making such a horrendous decision that ultimately caused what might be irreparable harm to his family. Certainly, his wife feels betrayed at the very least for living alongside her husband while he had the full knowledge that he had cheated on her and fathered a child because of it. How sad and tragic is that?

Other times, when people involve themselves in committing crimes, the only real thinking they may do about it is the kind of thinking that keeps them from getting caught. All too well are they aware of the potential consequences of their upcoming actions. In this case, as opposed to allowing moral law to dictate to them and keep them from breaking the law, they will use the determined consequences as a way to overcome the natural results of those actions. No one who commits a crime wants to go to jail, so they use their intelligence in an effort to commit the crime in such a way that they will not be caught. There, the consequences do not serve their natural purpose.

The moral realm is fraught with warning signs. We know we should not lie, for instance, because it cheats someone out of the truth. More than that, a person who lies perpetually tends to not remember all of their lies and will eventually get caught in one of them.

Isn't it interesting, though, that for the most part, decisions made in the amoral realm do not stress the way we *feel* about something. We busy ourselves going over all the facts and information we have at our disposal and make what we consider (and hope) to be an intelligent decision. Even so, at times, these decisions do not turn out to be the best for us – but there is no guarantee that they will be.

Those decisions within the moral realm are often made based primarily on the way we *feel* about something. It is here that we often rationalize things so that we wind up providing reasons for doing what we do or have done. This allows us to escape the feelings of guilt often associated with ignoring our consciences and doing what we should not do.

I can say this with almost 100% certainty, that the man I referred to who cheated on his wife and fathered a son wishes above all things that he could take it back and have a "do over." He probably thinks he would not have done what he did. That may or may not be true, but chances are that even if he had not done what he did on that particular day, he would have done it on another day because the only thing he used as a ruler in determining what his actions should be was how he *felt*.

We do the same thing in areas of religion. Actor Brad Pitt was recently quoted as saying that he was opposed to "strict religion." Having been raised in that atmosphere, he rejected it as an adult and favored another way of life. He now believes there is no God, nor is there any type of life after this life.

While Pitt might argue that he arrived at these decisions based on reason, the truth is that the catalyst for arriving where he arrived stemmed from how he felt about the way he was raised and what he experienced in the home. Bad or negative experiences create feelings that tend to warn us away from involvement in similar situations that will or can cause the same type of feelings.

When it comes to religion, politics, and areas of morality, feelings play a far larger role in arriving at decisions than reason or intellect. For instance, if more people read the Bible with an open mind, I fully believe that more people would respond positively to it and to God. This may not be the case, but knowing what I know about the Bible and its consistency, the case for it being authentic and truthful seems to be overwhelming to me. Others disagree with me, obviously, but it is interesting to see how many people become so vehemently opposed to the Bible and to Christianity. No other religion (with the possible exception of Judaism) creates this type of oppositional fervor. People can become very angry, and that anger is often unexplainable even by the individual exhibiting the anger. They don't know *why* they are angry. They just are angry. Obviously, something is triggered in them and they respond with vitriol at times. Why is this the case?

Most would say that it is due to the wrong they believe they have seen or heard of in the name of Christianity. History, they say, is proof enough that Christianity is wrong because of all the horrors perpetrated by people who have claimed to be Christians. This is no proof at all, except that it proves people can and do perform terrible things in the name of God or Christianity because they fail to understand the *truth* about Christianity.

It can be easily shown that people who perpetrate evils while stating that they are Christians are often not Christians at all. The person who would disagree with that statement does so not based on the biblical facts, but on how the facts of history make them *feel*.

All this is to say that within the realm of religion, most people respond to it because of how they feel. I personally have lost count of how many times I have heard statements like, "*I don't believe (feel) that a loving God would send people to hell*," as just one, for instance. A person who makes that claim does so because it angers or upsets them that the idea of an angry God casting people into a flaming pit exists at all. They repudiate such thinking because since that thinking makes them angry, it must be wrong. Again, they are basing their beliefs on their *feelings*.

This is why so many religions, philosophies, and ideologies exist today. However, when all is said and done, Christianity stands on one side of the aisle and all the rest reside on the other side. That may sound arrogant to suggest that Christianity stands alone, but the biblical facts attest to it. Stop and think about you and how you have arrived at the spot where you currently stand. I don't mean physically. I mean spiritually. How did you get there? What things prompted you to move along the path you have moved on and why do you now believe what you believe? Were actual facts involved in the process or platitudes and writings that prompted a "gut" reaction that made you smile and caused you to feel warm all over?

This is not to say that our reactions to facts cannot be good. It is to say that we cannot trust our feelings as the sole judge of the decisions we make. We simply cannot do that, yet this is exactly what we do most of the time, especially in the area of the moral realm.

THE CONCEPTION OF JESUS?

For most of us, we heard about Jesus because of the Bible. Whether we agree with its teachings or not doesn't matter. That was normally our first encounter with a testimony of Jesus' life, death, and resurrection.

Unfortunately, over time, other books have been written. These books claim to have inside knowledge about Jesus; who He was, how He lived, what caused His death, what actually happened at the resurrection, and much more.

Why Should We Believe Them?

These books have impacted a large segment of society and continue to do so. It has been estimated that over 1 million copies of *The Urantia Book* have been sold since it was first published in 1924. That's a lot of books, and that means that quite a few people have been either directly (if they read it) or indirectly (if they heard about it) affected by it.

If something has been read by this amount of people, then it obviously has something to say. So what *is* the message of *The Urantia Book* concerning Jesus? Can we trust that message? Let's find out.

Paper 120, titled "The Bestowal of Michael on Urantia," is alleged to have been written by Melchizadek, director of the revelatory commission. This paper essentially tells us about the entity *behind* the mortal Person of Jesus. That entity, according to this paper, is *Michael*. Apparently, it was Gabriel's job to oversee Michael's life on earth (Urantia) as Jesus.

At this point, let me quote the second paragraph of Paper 120 in order that the reader might get the sense of speech and flow which this Melchizadek uses to relate the events of Jesus' birth: "*Before the events I am about to delineate, Michael of Nebadon had bestowed himself six times after the similitude of six differing orders of his diverse creation of intelligent beings. Then he prepared to descend upon Urantia in the likeness of mortal flesh, the lowest order of his intelligent will creatures, and, as such a human of the material realm, to execute the final act in the drama of the acquirement of universe sovereignty in accordance with the mandates of the divine Paradise Rulers of the universe of universes.*"[14]

---

[14] *The Urantia Book, Paper 120,* Urantia Foundation (Chicago, 2010), 1323

Why Should We Believe Them?

That's a good deal of verbiage, and again, note that it is rendered to us in an almost science fiction type of speech that one would expect to hear from the latest Sci-Fi movie where normal earthlings meet up with beings from the Starbase Remulon of the Oxterior Lobe. We would expect them to talk like this because that is the way these types of beings have been presented to us over the years.

We have been ingrained to believe that highly intelligent beings and entities from other dimensions or worlds speak like this and it comes across as nearly being a bit painful for them to have to speak like this so that we understand. Obviously, their own native language is not at all like this, we assume, and therefore, having to *lower* themselves to be understood by us is something that they must force themselves to do. Because of that, it takes a good deal of verbiage to say what they are trying to say so that we understand it.

If you really break down that previously quoted paragraph, what we learn is that Michael went through the ranks on six different occasions from various culture groups in the universe. He then lowered himself by becoming a human being and living among people on the earth. He did this in order to fulfill the requirements set down by the Paradise Rulers. Look at how it was said in the original paragraph, though. Take just this sentence: "*...as such a human of the material realm, to execute the final act in the drama of the acquirement of universe sovereignty in accordance with the mandates of the divine Paradise Rulers.*" It certainly sounds intelligent, yet it's really a lot of hoopla over nothing. The bottom line is that supposedly Michael became a human being to fulfill the will of another in order to gain (regain?) title to the earth.

What does "the acquirement of universe sovereignty" actually mean? I don't know. I know what the individual words themselves mean, but when put together in such a fashion, it becomes a bit confusing. It's similar to when a person from another country begins to learn the language of their newly adopted country. Until they really get used to how the new language works, they wind up inadvertently making all sorts of grammatical errors. They use words that mean one thing, but they use them in a way that they should not be used. Because of that, it can almost be painful to listen to someone trying to learn their new language.

The Urantia Book is a book that purports to have been written by super-intelligent life from other worlds and other dimensions. I don't doubt that. What I doubt is their veracity based on the lack of ease in communicating with us.

As I read through it, at least some of the sentence structure is off, and there are too many run-on sentences and sentences that are more like fragments than anything else. Again, though, the book *reads* as if it was given to us straight from some high authority somewhere within the universe, and because of that, most people who find themselves fascinated by its revelatory nature will see that as merely a proof of its origin, as opposed to a question concerning its possibility of being fraudulent and deceitful.

The overriding problem, though, is that the heavy-handed verbiage makes the book appear *muddied*. In other words, the text, which is meant to *explain* and *enlighten*, often only succeeds in muddying the waters because it becomes at times difficult to sift through. Again, for many people, this works in the book's favor because of the impression that it is written by extremely intelligent individuals who are trying very hard to couch their words and tutelage in terms that we can understand.

The point of the first paragraph is that according to the book in question, Michael became the Jesus that actually lived on this earth, and it was all part of the divine plan to restore sovereignty to the entire universe. Had it been said as I just said it, it would hold no mystique and people would not be enamored with it. Because it sounds so ethereal, that fact tends to support its other-worldly origin.

The first part of Paper 120 continues by highlighting what Michael went through to become human and what it was like for him to live as a human being. Also according to *Urantia*, Michael was the one who decided to become human as Jesus, and it speaks of how Michael literally *became* sovereign through a series of acquisitions made by his bestowals. In essence, Michael became equal with deity because of the "bestowals" he went through. In essence, he grew into the role.

Throughout this paper, it becomes clear that Michael was the one who came up with the idea to become mortal, as Jesus, and to lower himself to reside among earthlings on this earth, otherwise known as Urantia.

Paragraph 9 of Paper 120 (page 1325) reveals that Michael was already in the position of "universe ruler" prior to taking on the role of "*Jesus of Nazareth (Christ Michael) on Urantia.*" God the Father, according to *Urantia,* is Paradise Father. In fact, there are many terms used throughout this paper and the rest of *The Urantia Book* that are very familiar to Christians. Labels and phrases like *Ancient of Days, Father, Immanuel,* and *Creator,* as well as numerous others, are littered throughout and serve to ease the mind of the reader by telling them they have entered into a realm that is familiar to them. However, it also serves to act as further revelation, going well beyond that which is incorporated in the Judeo-Christian Bible.

Because of this, people reading *The Urantia Book* and being at least familiar with the text of the Bible will come to believe that they have found a book that pulls back the curtain much further than the Bible does. This is exciting in and of itself for many and entices them to read much further and delve far more deeply in *The Urantia Book* than they would the Bible itself.

Why Should We Believe Them?

A few of the many things that Michael (as Jesus) is commissioned to do is explained for us in this quote, listed under the heading *The Bestowal Limitations*: *"As concerns the planet of your bestowal and the immediate generation of men living thereon at the time of your mortal sojourn, I counsel you to function largely in the role of a teacher. Give attention, first, to the liberation and inspiration of man's spiritual nature. Next, illuminate the darkened human intellect, heal the souls of men, and emancipate their minds from age-old fears. And then, in accordance with your mortal wisdom, minister to the physical well-being and material comfort of your brothers in the flesh. Live the ideal religious life for the inspiration and edification of all your universe."*[15]

We can almost see the pageantry occurring in the heavenlies as Michael was given one of several commissions in preparation for his role as Jesus, Savior to earth's people. Many of the statements used in the paragraphs following the one quoted above are simply a reiteration of what Jesus did while on earth. Yet at the same time, they sound far loftier than the Bible makes them out to be, and once again, this furthers the impression that their origin is far beyond this world.

The following paragraph is an interesting one, because it essentially takes its cue from Philippians 2, where we learn of how Jesus "emptied Himself," yet retained His full deity. *"I caution you ever to bear in mind that, while in fact you are to **become an ordinary human** of the realm, in potential **you will remain a Creator Son** of the Paradise Father. **Throughout this incarnation, although you will live and act as a Son of Man, the creative attributes of your personal divinity will follow you from Salvington to Urantia**. It will ever be within your power-of-will to terminate the incarnation at any moment subsequent to the arrival of your Thought Adjuster.*[16] *Prior to the arrival and*

---

[15] *The Urantia Book, Paper 120*, Urantia Foundation (Chicago, 2010), 1328
[16] The *Thought Adjuster* is Urantia's version of the Holy Spirit in Christianity.

reception of the Adjuster I will vouch for your personality integrity. But subsequent to the arrival of your Adjuster and concomitant with your progressive recognition of the nature and import of your bestowal mission, you should refrain from the formulation of any superhuman will-to-attainment, achievement, or power in view of the fact that your creator prerogatives will remain associated with your mortal personality because of the inseparability of these attributes from your personal presence. But no superhuman repercussions will attend your earthly career apart from the will of the Paradise Father unless you should, by an act of conscious and deliberate will, make an undivided decision which would terminate in whole-personality choice." (emphasis added)

If we can find our way through the forest of all that verbiage, it is interesting to note that the speaker says that Jesus (Michael) will become an ordinary human being while on earth. At the same time, his divine attributes will also be part of his life.

The troubling part is implied in the sentence that indicates that Michael as Jesus will always be able to cease his project at any point prior to the arrival of the "thought adjuster." In one sense, yes, Jesus could have done this and He notes it just prior to His arrest, trials, and execution. This occurred in the Garden of Gethsemane during Jesus' prayer time and just prior to His arrest, when the guards, led by Judas Iscariot, came to arrest Him. Jesus' words here were directed to Peter, who out of fear drew his sword and cut off one of the ears of a centurion. To this Jesus responded, *"Put up again thy sword into his place: for all they that take the sword shall perish with the sword. Thinkest thou that I cannot now pray to my Father, and he shall presently give me more than twelve legions of angels? But how then shall the scriptures be fulfilled, that thus it must be?"* (Matthew 26:52-54).

Why Should We Believe Them?

The truth of the matter is that had Jesus at any point rejected His role in the plan of redemption, the Scriptures would have gone unfulfilled. Had that happened, God would have been made out to be a liar. Since God cannot lie (cf. Titus 1:2), there was no way that could happen.

The Urantia Book would have us believe that Michael (as Jesus) could have changed His mind at any point prior to receiving the Thought Adjuster. This would have left Scripture unfulfilled and that could not occur.

The Urantia Book makes it clear that Jesus was God *incarnate;* however, it needs to be understood that God has a unique definition as far as the teachings of Urantia are concerned. Moreover, it is also clear that Jesus did not exist until Michael became him through the incarnation process as taught in *The Urantia Book.* Yet Scripture teaches that Jesus was *always* the Eternal Son, fully equal with God the Father (cf. John 1:1-4).

This does not present a problem for adherents of Urantia teaching because of their unique definition of God. It *does* present a problem for Christians who believe that *The Urantia Book* may contain truth.

It is truly interesting that *The Urantia Book*, rather than dispute the teachings of the Bible, often not only coincides with it, but adds detail *to* it. For instance, we do not know why God chose Joseph and Mary to be Jesus' earthly parents, as far as the Bible is concerned. That decision was made within the counsel of the Godhead prior to earth's foundation.

The Urantia Book tells us why the parentage of Jesus, humanly speaking, fell to Joseph and Mary. We also learn why Michael allegedly decided on that particular time frame to enter into earth's society, and why earth was chosen at all. *"Of all couples living in Palestine at about the time of Michael's projected bestowal, Joseph and Mary possessed the most ideal combination of widespread racial connections and superior average of personality endowments. It was the plan of Michael to appear on earth as an average man, that the common people might understand him and receive him; wherefore Gabriel selected just such persons as Joseph and Mary to become the bestowal parents."*[17]

As we progress through the pages of *The Urantia Book*, we do begin to learn that apparently much of what has been connected to Jesus from the Old Testament has been misapplied. Rather than denigrate those who have done this, the information is simply presented in a matter-of-fact way. By the way, it is interesting that those from Urantia call the Old Testament just that, as opposed to the Tanakh or Torah.

"Most of the so-called Messianic prophecies of the Old Testament were made to apply to Jesus long after his life had been lived on earth. For centuries the Hebrew prophets had proclaimed the coming of a deliverer, and these promises had been construed by successive generations as referring to a new Jewish ruler who would sit upon the throne of David and, by the reputed miraculous methods of Moses, proceed to establish the Jews in Palestine as a powerful nation, free from all foreign domination. Again, many figurative passages found throughout the Hebrew scriptures were subsequently misapplied to the life mission of Jesus. Many Old Testament sayings were so distorted as to appear to fit some episode of the Master's earth life. Jesus himself onetime publicly denied any connection with the royal house of David."[18]

With respect to the last sentence in the quote above, nothing is provided as a source, so the reader is left to assume that either the speaker there was referencing some obscure passage of Scripture or

---

[17] *The Urantia Book, Paper 122*, Urantia Foundation (Chicago, 2010), 1345
[18] Ibid, 1347-8

simply saying it happened, but it did so outside of the actual record of Scripture.

This next quote attempts to cast doubt on the virgin birth of Christ: *"Even the passage, "a maiden shall bear a son," was made to read, "a virgin shall bear a son." This was also true of the many genealogies of both Joseph and Mary which were constructed subsequent to Michael's career on earth. Many of these lineages contain much of the Master's ancestry, but on the whole they are not genuine and may not be depended upon as factual. The early followers of Jesus all too often succumbed to the temptation to make all the olden prophetic utterances appear to find fulfillment in the life of their Lord and Master."*[19]

With respect to Mary being a "maiden" or a "virgin," the truth is simple. The text being referred to in the quote above is found in Isaiah 7:1-17. This section is often referred to as *Book of Immanuel*. The controversy that arose stems from the use of the Hebrew word *almah*. Fruchtenbaum believes that Isaiah 7:13-17 *"contains two separate prophecies with different purposes, and having different fulfillments at different times."*[20]

As stated, the main problem is related to the meaning of the word *almah*. This word – according to Fruchtenbaum – means *a virgin, a young virgin, a virgin of marriageable age,* and it *"is used seven times in the Hebrew Scriptures and not once is it used to describe a married woman; this point is not debated."*[21]

Fruchtenbaum then points out a number of places in Scripture where this word – *almah* – is used specifically *for* a virgin. Genesis 24:43, Exodus 2:8, Psalm 68:25, Song of Songs 1:3; 6:8, Proverbs 30:18-19,

---

[19] *The Urantia Book, Paper 122*, Urantia Foundation (Chicago, 2010), 1348
[20] Arnold Fruchtenbaum, *Messianic Christology*, (Ariel Ministries, 1998), 33
[21] Ibid, 34

and finally in Isaiah 7:14. Fruchtenbaum's point is simple. *"Since all of the [first six] verses mean 'a virgin,' what reason is there for making Isaiah 7:14 the only exception?"*[22] Certainly this makes sense, but to further clarify, he asks an important question: *"if the woman in Isaiah 7:14 were a non-virgin, then God would be promising a sign involving fornication and illegitimacy. It is unthinkable that God would sanction sin, and in any case, what would be so unusual about an illegitimate baby that could possibly constitute a sign? As far as ancient Jewish writers were concerned, there was no argument about Isaiah 7:14 predicting a virgin birth. The* Septuagint *is a Greek translation of the Hebrew Scriptures made about 200 B.C., 200 years before the issue of Jesus' Messiahship ever arose. The Jews who made this translation, living much closer to the times of Isaiah than we do today, translated Isaiah 7:14 using the Greek word* parthenos *which very clearly and exclusively means a virgin. There can therefore be no doubt that the unique event which God is promising as a sign, is the miraculous conception of a son by a girl who is still a virgin."*[23]

Of course, that is Fruchtenbaum's opinion vs. the opinion provided in *The Urantia Book*. Either the beings who wrote that book were taking a shot at the virgin birth and the direct line of ancestry to David, or they are telling the truth. Let's ask another question. Why does it matter to those entities who provided *The Urantia Book* to people of this world? What possible reason could it matter to them whether or not people of the earth who believe the information presented in *The Urantia Book* think that Jesus was born of a virgin or not?

In fact, wouldn't it serve their purposes far better to have people continue to believe that the events surrounding Jesus' conception and eventual birth were altogether supernatural? The reality seems to be

---

[22] Arnold Fruchtenbaum, *Messianic Christology*, (Ariel Ministries, 1998), 34
[23] Ibid, 34-5

that the beings speaking in the *The Urantia Book* are trying to cast doubt on Jesus' credentials without coming out and saying it. They are doing so by placing the blame on His followers and others who came *after* Jesus. This is an intelligent way to attack the truths of orthodox Christianity without denigrating Jesus Himself. After all, it is implied, it's not Jesus' fault that some of His followers adapted many of the Old Testament Scriptures and wrongly applied them to Jesus. It is also not Jesus' fault that a major misconception was allegedly made with the impression of the virgin birth.

The problem actually is bigger than that. What these entities who wrote *The Urantia Book* are doing is actually denigrating the Bible, yet the gospels are *narrative accounts* of events that purportedly happened. Yes, they were written *after* Jesus lived, died, and rose again, but that does not obscure the truth of the matter, nor does it negate the truth that is seen in those narratives.

Luke, for instance, did a tremendous amount of research before he put pen to paper, as it were, to bring out the truth of the matter. In Luke 1:1-3 we read, "*Forasmuch as many have taken in hand to set forth in order a declaration of those things which are most surely believed among us, Even as they delivered them unto us, which from the beginning were eyewitnesses, and ministers of the word; It seemed good to me also, having had perfect understanding of all things from the very first, to write unto thee in order, most excellent Theophilus.*"

Luke wrote from information he received from eyewitnesses after interviewing them thoroughly. For instance, in Luke 2:10-14, we read these words: "*And the angel said unto them, Fear not: for, behold, I bring you good tidings of great joy, which shall be to all people. For unto you is born this day in the city of David a Saviour, which is Christ the Lord. And this shall be a sign unto you; Ye shall find the babe wrapped in swaddling clothes, lying in a manger.*

And suddenly there was with the angel a multitude of the heavenly host praising God, and saying, Glory to God in the highest, and on earth peace, good will toward men."

If we take the word of *The Urantia Book*, what they are saying is that after the fact, people created a story in which angels came and announced the birth of Jesus, the Savior, to the shepherds. At least part of what the angel announces refers back to Isaiah 7. That was God's sign and according to Luke, that event happened, announced to the shepherds by angels. If we disagree with that, then we have to say that it did *not* happen, but was made up and inserted into the biblical record to prop up Jesus' credentials.

What *The Urantia Book* teaches is that Jesus' qualifications as Savior and Messiah are a bit lacking and He was not, in fact, born of a virgin. In actuality, this makes little sense from the perspective of entities and beings that are supposedly so enlightened and intelligent. Why wouldn't Michael, if he was actually *incarnated* (as *The Urantia Book* teaches) as Jesus, be conceived in a miraculous way such as that described in the Bible? If he was simply born the way the rest of us are born (without divine intervention), then the question arises as to his actual and supposed deity when he (Michael) allegedly became Jesus.

Does it not stand to reason that if Michael as Jesus was born the way the rest of us are born, in order for Michael to incarnate himself as Jesus, he would actually have to *possess* or indwell the human body of Jesus *after* Jesus was born, with Jesus having His own soul? Again, this makes little sense.

The fact that *The Urantia Book* teaches that there was no miracle surrounding the conception of Michael as Jesus is one of the strongest arguments against it being the truth! Here we have an allegedly enlightened, superior being among a multitude of beings far beyond our dimension and realm. Since Michael already existed (as taught in *The*

Urantia Book), then how does one actually incarnate himself into his own human body that will be created under normal human coitus?

I quoted a paragraph that states that the "thought adjuster" would not arrive to Michael's human body (as Jesus) immediately. So exactly *how* did Michael *become* Jesus if the normal conception allegedly took place between Joseph and Mary? It couldn't have, unless Michael separately simply *possessed* the human body of Jesus. In that case, he would not literally be part of Jesus' make-up or even part of his personality. He would simply be *residing* inside the human body of Jesus who would have had his own personality, his own character, and his own DNA, which he would have gained from the sexual union of his two earthly parents.

In my view, there is a huge hole here in the reasoning of these entities who gave us *The Urantia Book*. While the average person might not notice that hole, it is nonetheless there, and it looms large over the entire issue of the virgin birth and the alleged deity of Archangel Michael.

Paper 122 continues with a great many details about Joseph and Mary, their early lives, their education, and their stations in life. It then continues with Joseph and Mary as adults and how their characters and personalities contributed to that of Jesus. Interestingly enough, the detail that is provided in *The Urantia Book* extends to the type of dishes they owned and what their one-room house looked like.

Whether true or not, this type of information tends to add to a perceived truthfulness with respect to *The Urantia Book*, that much is clear. Along the way, however, the writers of the book try at times to negate the veracity of Scripture, doing so in such a matter of fact way that few would question it.

For instance, we all know from Matthew 1 that the lineage of Joseph is traced directly back to King David. Yet *The Urantia Book* informs us that Joseph was *not* a direct descendent of David, and in fact, had certain Gentile strains within him. Who do we believe? That's up to you, of course, but I see no reason to discount Scripture simply because some alleged *ascended master* says otherwise.

Again, we are aware of the fact that Jesus was actually born in the town of Bethlehem (cf. Matthew 2). Moreover, the gospel of Luke tells us that at one point, Caesar Augustus decreed that everyone should return to their home town to be registered and numbered in order to have an accurate census and a tax base for the Roman Empire (cf. Luke 2).

This is exactly *why* Jesus was born in Bethlehem. It was due to the fact that Joseph and Mary had to go there because of Augustus' decree. Luke 2:6 states quite clearly, *"And so it was, that, while they were there, the days were accomplished that she should be delivered."* The text obviously tells us that they were there ("while they were there") and her pregnancy came to the end and she gave birth to a baby boy they named Jesus.

Here is what *The Urantia Book* tells us about this event and the *real* reason Mary chose to go with Joseph. *"It was not necessary that Mary should go to Bethlehem for enrollment — Joseph was authorized to register for his family — but Mary, being an adventurous and aggressive person, insisted on accompanying him. She feared being left alone lest the child be born while Joseph was away, and again, Bethlehem being not far from the City of Judah, Mary foresaw a possible pleasurable visit with her kinswoman Elizabeth.*

"Joseph virtually forbade Mary to accompany him, but it was of no avail; when the food was packed for the trip of three or four days, she prepared double rations and made ready for the journey. But before

they actually set forth, Joseph was reconciled to Mary's going along, and they cheerfully departed from Nazareth at the break of day."[24]

While it makes for great fiction, the truth comes into question here. Mary is presented in Scripture as being someone who is completely humble. We need only go back one chapter to Luke 1 to learn her response when told of her impending pregnancy by Gabriel. *"And Mary said, Behold the handmaid of the Lord; be it unto me according to thy word. And the angel departed from her"* (v. 38).

How is it that Mary is seen as being humble here, but when it comes to her husband, she is presented as being "adventurous and aggressive"? That does not even compute, yet that is what we are told in *The Urantia Book*. At this point, some will attempt to marry the idea of humility with being adventurous and aggressive, but it is impossible to do. A truly humble person might have strong convictions, but that does not mean that person seeks to overrule another, especially in a marital relationship where within the culture of Judaism, the husband was the head of the home.

---

[24] *The Urantia Book, Paper 122,* Urantia Foundation (Chicago, 2010), 1350

Why Should We Believe Them?

A YOUNG BOY

M oving from the conception and birth of Jesus, *The Urantia Book* moves us right along to witness the early years of Jesus, something that the Bible itself is silent on, with the exception of our Lord's visit to the Temple at the age of twelve. We know from the biblical narrative that by the time Jesus reached this age, He was intelligent and wise enough to impress the teachers and rulers at the synagogue (cf. Luke 2:46-52).

According to *The Urantia Book* Jesus spent a few years in Egypt with his parents, Joseph and Mary. There, they visited relatives, and it was apparently during this time that Jesus was given a copy of the Greek translation of the Hebrew Scriptures (the Septuagint). Again, there is nothing about this in the Bible and it seems clear to me that God left out the details of Jesus' early life except those that were pertinent for our greater understanding and those which enabled us to see a number of the prophecies that were fulfilled by Jesus as well as others like Herod.

The amount of extraneous detail included in *The Urantia Book* is interesting if not amusing. We learn that Joseph never really believed that Jesus would grow up to be a king who would deliver Israel, yet in another portion of *The Urantia Book* we are told that had Joseph lived longer, he would no doubt have come to believe in Jesus' own mission. Well, which was it, and what proof is offered in *The Urantia Book* that would verify these statements? None.

The Urantia Book informs us of certain events that occurred in the life of Jesus at the age of nine. Apparently, Jesus was not only a model student, but an artist as well. His interest in art got him in trouble, apparently. *"The most serious trouble as yet to come up at school occurred in late winter when Jesus dared to challenge the chazan regarding the teaching that **all images, pictures, and drawings were idolatrous in nature**. Jesus delighted in drawing landscapes as well as in modeling a great variety of objects in potter's clay. **Everything of that sort was strictly forbidden by Jewish law**, but up to this time he had managed to disarm his parents' objection to such an extent that they had permitted him to continue in these activities."*[25] (emphasis added)

---

[25] *The Urantia Book, Paper 124*, Urantia Foundation (Chicago, 2010), 1366

Why Should We Believe Them?

This is typical of *The Urantia Book* in making statements that have no adjoining source. For someone to simply read the above quote giving specific attention to the bold font, one would read it and believe it because it *sounds* reasonable. After all, at least one of the Ten Commandments tells us to avoid idolatry (cf. Exodus 10:4, 23).

The blanket statement made in *The Urantia Book* severely stretches the truth of the matter. Essentially, within Judaism and the Bible, art was "*the working out of the laws of beauty in the construction of things, [and] is regarded in the Bible as wisdom resulting from divine inspiration.*"[26] While it is clear that idolatry was always to be avoided, this did not stop craftsmen from creating objects of beauty, not for worship, but simply to be pleasing to the eyes.

As far as rabbinic tradition goes, "*Rabbis forbade only the fashioning of the four figures of Ezekiel as a whole or of any other angelic being, and especially the making of human figures, as these might be made objects of worship.*"[27] This would seem to negate the previous quote from *The Urantia Book*. Moreover, "*Portrait-painting, therefore, was never forbidden by the Law.*"[28]

Someone has their wires crossed. Is it the entities who produced *The Urantia Book* or is the mix-up somewhere else? While many synagogues (ancient and modern) seem to be devoid of art, the reason for this is a pragmatic one. Many believe art in the sanctuary tends to detract from the worship experience by potentially distracting the worshiper.

The interesting thing about *The Urantia Book* lies in the fact that Jesus is often made to look *too* human. By that it is meant that in at

---

[26] http://www.jewishencyclopedia.com/view.jsp?artid=1823&letter=A#ixzz1MlGVmHME
[27] Ibid
[28] Ibid

least some cases, the way he reacts to a situation (as seen in the narration of *The Urantia Book*) borders on sinful activity. As the tale unfolds regarding Jesus' continued enjoyment of art and particularly drawing, under reprimand, he steps up and takes his adult accusers to task, something he would never have done as a young boy; unless, of course, we say that the very things Jesus (as well as Paul and others) taught in Scripture did not apply to Jesus Himself. That of course is an absurd characterization.

As I write this, I am beginning to realize why *The Urantia Book* may have not dealt with the actual life of Jesus until the very end of its nearly 2,100 pages. Consider that by the time a person gets to the end, provided that they started at the beginning and simply read straight through, they would have absorbed a great deal of what I certainly consider to be false teaching.

Traversing through all previous parts and finally reaching part five of *The Urantia Book* has given the reader much time to be influenced by the deceit that runs throughout the book. Yes, I call it deceit because that's exactly what I believe it to be and will not make any bones about it.

Essentially, then, upon arriving at approximately page 1,350, the reader has already been quite indoctrinated in the thinking of the entities that created *The Urantia Book,* and because of that, may have largely and subconsciously adopted the thinking put forth in the book.

So to that person, Jesus then is seen in a very refreshing light. Altogether he is very wise, yet capable of experiencing frustration toward his elders, as a young person. Because of that, he is also quite capable of confronting them and, in essence, demanding that he be treated fairly. Since most people know of the fact (whether the details were ever learned, or were learned and escaped them) that Jesus in the Bible often went head to head with the Pharisees and religious leaders, the idea that he went head to head with his teachers as a nine-year-old boy does not seem out of the ordinary. In fact, it seems very much in keeping with the type of man he is portrayed as being in the Bible.

By the way, before I go any further, let me point out what the reader may have already noticed. The terminology and phraseology utilized in this fifth part of *The Urantia Book* is completely different than other parts of the book.

Recall earlier that I pointed out the tendency of the narration to become overburdened by additional verbiage that served to muddy things up a bit. In this fifth section of *The Urantia Book,* this does not at all seem to be the case. Obviously, it appears as though the writer(s) of this entire part (Midway Commission) are entirely different from Melchizadek.

In this part of *The Urantia Book*, the narrative is much more fluid and even lighthearted. In spite of this type of presentation, facts are facts, and it would appear that many facts are either omitted or glossed over by Midway Commission as they tell the tale of Jesus leading up to the age of twelve when we read of Him in the biblical account at the Temple.

Interestingly enough, the account of Jesus at the Temple in Jerusalem (cf. Luke 2) is not included in the *The Urantia Book* narrative until the age of thirteen, not as the biblical account informs us, while Jesus was twelve. While there, he is said to have rejected certain aspects of Judaism for a more all-encompassing view of God that superseded the Law of Moses. Specifically, Jesus is said to have rejected, at this juncture, the concept of a wrathful God.

"Jesus simply would not accept explanations of worship and religious devotion which involved belief in the wrath of God or the anger of the Almighty. In further discussion of these questions, after the conclusion

of the temple visit, when his father became mildly insistent that he acknowledge acceptance of the orthodox Jewish beliefs, Jesus turned suddenly upon his parents and, looking appealingly into the eyes of his father, said: 'My father, it cannot be true — the Father in heaven cannot so regard his erring children on earth. The heavenly Father cannot love his children less than you love me. And I well know, no matter what unwise thing I might do, you would never pour out wrath upon me nor vent anger against me. If you, my earthly father, possess such human reflections of the Divine, how much more must the heavenly Father be filled with goodness and overflowing with mercy. I refuse to believe that my Father in heaven loves me less than my father on earth'."[29]

While this sounds gracious, loving, and even exceptionally selfless, it is either true or false. It is clear that in the Bible, Jesus spoke often of eternal torment of those who die in their sin. To die in your sin means to die without receiving the salvation that Jesus has made available to humanity. Though people disagree over the concept that a loving God would allow people to choose hell as their eternal destiny, the Bible is very clear on the subject. The only way to get around that clarity is to allegorize Jesus' teachings.

So what we are left with (again) is the decision to either accept the Bible as truth or *The Urantia Book* as truth. Since they contradict one another, they cannot both be true, and since we know that there can only be one truth, it can only be contained within Scripture or in *The Urantia Book*.

---

[29] *The Urantia Book, Paper 125*, Urantia Foundation (Chicago, 2010), 1378

WHAT HAPPENED NEXT

The Urantia Book describes two specific years of Jesus' life – years fourteen and fifteen – as unique and important. This is interesting because of course the Bible itself makes no such boast or claim. In essence, it can be assumed from the biblical record that every year of Jesus' life was equally as important as the next.

What we see in Scripture – at Jesus' birth or His time in the Temple when his parents looked frantically for Him – are events that God wanted us to know about. These events are just as important as the other events in His life that we do *not* know about and apparently do not need to know about, either.

It is like the event of Jesus' baptism by John the Baptist. That was a very important event. So also was the event immediately occurring after that in which the Holy Spirit led Jesus into the wilderness so that He could be tempted by Satan over a period of forty days and forty nights.

We learn from at least one of the gospel writers that Jesus performed many miracles and did many things that would fill volumes of books well beyond what we recognize as the Bible of the Christian faith. While those events are obviously important, it is enough that we have the record of what God chose to give us.

But let's return to *The Urantia Book* to see what it is we are to learn about Jesus that allegedly took place during His fourteenth and fifteenth year of life on this planet. The authors of *The Urantia Book* tell us that *"OF ALL Jesus' earth-life experiences, the fourteenth and fifteenth years were the most crucial. These two years, after he began to be self-conscious of divinity and destiny, and before he achieved a large measure of communication with his indwelling Adjuster, were the most trying of his eventful life on Urantia. It is this period of two years which should be called the great test, the real temptation. No human youth, in passing through the early confusions and adjustment problems of adolescence, ever experienced a more crucial testing than that which Jesus passed through during his transition from childhood to young manhood."*[30]

What is of course interesting above all else is the way *The Urantia Book* manages to provide details of Jesus' life seemingly year-by-year where the Bible is essentially silent. This undoubtedly serves to once

---

[30] *The Urantia Book, Paper 126*, Urantia Foundation (Chicago, 2010), 1386

again speak of the truthfulness of the book. Yet there is nothing outside of Scripture that I am aware of that would offer any type of verification for it. In fact, many critics of Scripture will argue that there is precious little outside of Scripture that provides affirmation of Scripture itself, but there *is* at least some information available.

The Urantia Book goes well beyond the bounds of Scripture, providing significant details of the life of Jesus as well as many other areas. Because these incidents are presented as fact, there must be a way to verify them at least to some degree.

But let's argue that there is nothing verifiable outside of Scripture for what takes place *within* Scripture. The one large difference between the Bible and *The Urantia Book* is that it routinely tells us what Jesus was thinking and/or feeling. This is done occasionally in the Bible, but not to any great degree. *The Urantia Book* regularly provides a narrative that includes "insider knowledge" as it were for the reader, and once again, this will serve to bolster the argument that *The Urantia Book* is truly a book of supernatural origin, whereas the Bible is at most a truncated version of what aliens/ascended masters were attempting to reveal to us, but too many of Jesus' followers simply got things wrong.

According to the narrative within *The Urantia Book*, we learn that to His parents, Jesus became an enigma. They were unable to understand Him and though they believed that at least to some degree He was remarkable and would do remarkable things, there was nothing out of the ordinary that seemed to verify that belief. There were no miracles that they could point to and nothing beyond His own personality and character that offered them a look beyond the veil, so to speak.

Apparently, on September 25th – a Tuesday, according to *The Urantia Book* – Joseph had an accident at work and died. This resulted in an attitude in Jesus that is hard to imagine. *"Jesus cheerfully accepted the responsibilities so suddenly thrust upon him, and he carried them faithfully to the end. At least one great problem and anticipated difficulty in his life had been tragically solved — he would not now be expected to go to Jerusalem to study under the rabbis. It remained always true that Jesus 'sat at no man's feet.' He was ever willing to learn from even the humblest of little children, but he never derived authority to teach truth from human sources."*[31]

There is no mention of Jesus spending any time in mourning, but instead we see Him "cheerfully" understanding His new role as head of the home. That makes little sense, if we consider that Jesus cried at the death of His own friend Lazarus just prior to raising Him from the dead (cf. John 11).

During Jesus' fifteenth year, He allegedly came across the Book of Enoch and from that book chose the label "son of man" for Himself, at least as far as *The Urantia Book* tells it. Essentially, what we learn from *The Urantia Book* is that Jesus *grew* into an understanding of His mission. Yet the Bible seems to indicate that He clearly understood His mission from an early age. His comment to His parents at the age of twelve – that He had to be about His Father's business – is one such way in which we understand that He was aware of something far deeper about His own life, His purpose, His mission, and the road ahead of Him.

Certainly, as a baby, He likely had little comprehension of this fact, and that probably extended into the time of being a toddler. As He grew, His intellect was certainly able to grasp the portent and meaning of His life on earth.

However, the way *The Urantia Book* presents it is actually nothing different than what many esoteric books and writings try to do with-

---

[31] *The Urantia Book, Paper 126*, Urantia Foundation (Chicago, 2010), 1388

in the confines of the New Age movement. They try to bring Jesus down purely to our level, as a human being *primarily*. Yes, many within the New Age will admit freely that Jesus *became* a god by unlocking His own potential, a potential that we all share. This is far different from admitting that Jesus was and remains God – as John 1:1-4 states – because it *removes* His deity from Him until such a time as He was able to understand that He was the first among many to release His inner divinity, and because of that would become a pattern for many.

The Urantia Book is a book about the New Age. It is a handbook that is designed to show people what they are and how to achieve as Jesus achieved. Everything so far within *The Urantia Book* indicates that Jesus, while special – having been Archangel Michael incarnated – was really little more than a pattern for the rest of the world to copy. Michael – as Jesus – showed us the way. We follow that same pattern and arrive at the same stated goal as Jesus did.

MITHRAISM

Skipping ahead several sections in *The Urantia Book*, we learn about the way in which the various religions of the world were understood and catalogued by a young contemporary of Jesus named Ganid. First up in *The Urantia Book* is a short section on Cynicism, and apparently that system is to be lauded as retaining much of the flavor of the Melchizadekian influences and teachings.

Judaism is listed next, and apparently both Jesus and Ganid took some of the teachings and compiled them with other teachings from various religious systems. What is essentially implied here is that unlike what the Bible teaches, Judaism was not a system of worship created by God and the Jews were not a special people created by God. They are merely one among many. In fact, *The Urantia Book* makes it a point to mention that the Jews simply took from many religions and wound up creating their own, ultimately filtering things down from many gods to one God.[32]

The Urantia Book also notates the various terms used for God within the Jewish faith and explains what those specific names mean.

It should come as no surprise that Buddhism seemed to be the closest to authentic *religion* as far as *The Urantia Book* is concerned. It should also be no surprise that Buddhism is much closer to the New Age system of non-religion as you can get without being overtly religious.

Hinduism is next, and of course what we understand here is that within all of these systems compiled by Jesus and Ganid there is a thread that connects them all, one to another. They do not stand alone, but are interconnected. In essence, *The Urantia Book* is trying to say that all of these religious systems stem from the same origin, but are simply changed or modified to suit the individual people groups throughout the world since the beginning.

The unifying factor in all of these systems is Melchizadek. This is true of the next system referred to as Zorastrianism. *The Urantia Book* connects the dots of Zorastrianism back to Melchizadek via Judaism.

We continue along the religious trail through Suduanism (Jainism), Shinto, Taoism, and Confusianism, finally arriving at something

---

[32] *The Urantia Book, Paper 96*, Urantia Foundation (Chicago, 2010), 1052

called "Our Religion" (in quotes). This turns out to be a synthesis of systems that both Jesus and Ganid decreed would become their own personal religion. Essentially, this was done when Ganid formulated what he believed were the teachings of Jesus.

The next paper in *The Urantia Book* is number 132, and here it defines Jesus' sojourn in Rome. It is also here that Jesus apparently encountered a number of religious orders, but seemed to be most taken with a group known as the Mithraic group, or Mithraism.

I have long heard many people claim that Christianity was simply an adopted form of Mithraism, and in *The Urantia Book* that point is made clear. There have been a number of well-researched books written by individuals who have refuted that, but those who prefer to believe that Christianity is nothing but an adapted form of Mithraism will not be satisfied with any book that seeks to dispute what *The Urantia Book* states.

I would like, however, to direct the reader to one particular book titled *The Roman Cult of Mithras* by Manfred Clauss (and translated by Richard Gordon). This particular book is highly regarded and *"has become widely accepted as the most reliable, and readable, account of this fascinating subject."*[33]

It is interesting to note that by all accounts, the earliest form of Mithraism was not seen in the Roman world until toward the very end of the first century. This fact alone makes it impossible for Jesus to have run into people from this group, since it did not exist during His lifetime. Yet, *The Urantia Book* tells us otherwise. Facts are facts and Clauss seems to have done his homework, providing archaeological evidence that the first artifact of Mithraism is dated to a time just prior to A.D. 90 in the form of an inscription on a statue, and

---

[33] Manfred Clauss, *The Roman Cult of Mithras* (New York, 2000, back cover

that the cult itself did not originally form in Rome, but in outlying provinces.

In truth, we also know that many Christian churches were built *over* caves and areas where Mithraism existed. This was not done as a way to *absorb* the teachings, but to stamp them out. According to Clauss, by the end of the fourth century, Mithraism was all but gone, yet *The Urantia Book* provides us with a different story altogether.

We have the actual historical facts that indicate to us that Mithraism was a cult that developed toward the end of the first century, was opposed by Christianity, and died a natural death, so to speak, by the end of the fourth century. Its lifespan was just under three centuries.

The Urantia Book continues with what appears to be more fabrications telling us that Jesus met a Stoic named Angamon, who also ultimately became a dear friend of the apostle Paul. One of the major things that Jesus allegedly taught Angamon had to do with the ascending mortal. *"The standard of true values must be looked for in the spiritual world and on divine levels of eternal reality. To an ascending mortal all lower and material standards must be recognized as transient, partial, and inferior. The scientist, as such, is limited to the discovery of the relatedness of material facts. Technically, he has no right to assert that he is either materialist or idealist, for in so doing he has assumed to forsake the attitude of a true scientist since any and all such assertions of attitude are the very essence of philosophy."*[34]

Notice that here, Jesus appears to be teaching exactly what much of the New Age teaches. Yet, when we read Scripture, we see nothing of this type of teaching. In fact, Jesus did not talk like this at all in the Bible. *"The standard of true values must be looked for in the spiritual world and on divine levels of eternal reality."* There is nothing in the

---

[34] *The Urantia Book, Paper 132*, Urantia Foundation (Chicago, 2010), 1457

Bible that even remotely resembles that pattern of speech from Jesus' lips. It's simply not there, so once again, people will need to decide whether the Bible is the truth, or whether *The Urantia Book* is engaged in expressing it.

Jesus also apparently taught that truth is relative, if we believe *The Urantia Book*. "*Goodness, like truth, is always relative and unfailingly evil-contrasted. It is the perception of these qualities of goodness and truth that enables the evolving souls of men to make those personal decisions of choice which are essential to eternal survival.*"[35] These are words that *The Urantia Book* states Jesus said to a man named Mardus, who was the recognized leader of the Cynics based in Rome.

This then is an obvious contradiction with the truth of the Bible. Jesus never taught or implied that truth is relative. He said of Himself, "*I am the way, the truth, and the life*" (cf. John 14:6), and it would be impossible to state that if truth was in fact *relative*. If truth is always a moving platter of options based on a given situation, then truth is literally up for grabs, and this was noted at the beginning of this book.

The more I read *The Urantia Book*, the clearer the lie becomes. In fact, it is so plain that it is impossible to not see it or ignore it. The tragedy here is that people read *The Urantia Book* and accept it as truth, in spite of the fact that contradictions are replete throughout the text.

---

[35] *The Urantia Book, Paper 132,* Urantia Foundation (Chicago, 2010), 1457

Why Should We Believe Them?

DEATH AND RESURRECTION

Interestingly enough, the trial of Jesus, His death and even His resurrection read enough like the Scriptures in *Urantia*, except there are also parts where large embellishments occur. This is evident during the time before His trial while in Gethsemane, His trial, and His crucifixion.

If someone were to simply pick up *The Urantia Book* and read the narrative of Jesus' crucifixion without having previous biblical knowledge of it, and then read the biblical version, they would probably find little to nothing out of the ordinary. However, in truth, there is an implicit tone to the narrative that is decidedly different from the tone of Scripture, and that tone was something that pointedly references His humanity more than His deity.

During the time between the death and resurrection of Jesus, preparations were apparently made by the ascended beings, and they prepared Jesus' mortal body for His time in *morontia*. In short, "*Morontia is the realm between the material and the spiritual.*"[36] It was also at this time that Archangel Michael disassociated himself spiritually from the mortal body of Jesus.

In effect, what *The Urantia Book* teaches is that it was not Jesus' actual physical form (as we would think of physical), but it was His *morontia* form that came out of the tomb. In fact, we are told that Jesus' actual physical body was still back in the tomb, lying where it had been placed.

Christians, of course, believe that when Jesus rose from the dead, He rose with the very physical body which He had been born into some thirty or so years prior. The only thing He left in the tomb was the shroud that covered Him, along with the sudarium, which had been used as a covering for His head.

However, once again *The Urantia Book* explains Jesus' resurrection in quite another way. "*The Christian belief in the resurrection of Jesus has been based on the fact of the 'empty tomb.' It was indeed a fact that the tomb was empty, but this is not the truth of the resurrection. The tomb was truly empty when the first believers arrived, and this fact, associated with that of the undoubted resurrection of the Master, led to the formulation of a belief which was not true: the teaching that the*

---

[36] http://www.urantia.org/en/topical-studies/morontia-life

material and mortal body of Jesus was raised from the grave. Truth having to do with spiritual realities and eternal values cannot always be built up by a combination of apparent facts. Although individual facts may be materially true, it does not follow that the association of a group of facts must necessarily lead to truthful spiritual conclusions.

"The tomb of Joseph was empty, not because the body of Jesus had been rehabilitated or resurrected, but because the celestial hosts had been granted their request to afford it a special and unique dissolution, a return of the "dust to dust," without the intervention of the delays of time and without the operation of the ordinary and visible processes of mortal decay and material corruption.

"The mortal remains of Jesus underwent the same natural process of elemental disintegration as characterizes all human bodies on earth except that, in point of time, this natural mode of dissolution was greatly accelerated, hastened to that point where it became well-nigh instantaneous.

"The true evidences of the resurrection of Michael are spiritual in nature, albeit this teaching is corroborated by the testimony of many mortals of the realm who met, recognized, and communed with the resurrected morontia Master. He became a part of the personal experience of almost one thousand human beings before he finally took leave of Urantia."[37]

Of course, it is to Satan's advantage that this version is the one that is believed. If only it were true, as far as Satan was concerned! Had that been the case, then the promises of God would have utterly failed and Satan would be the victor. As it stands, because Jesus rose bodily (physically) from the grave, He literally conquered death because death was not able to keep Him in the grave.

---

[37] *The Urantia Book, Paper 189,* Urantia Foundation (Chicago, 2010), 2023-4

Why Should We Believe Them?

11

LAST THOUGHTS ABOUT URANTIA

When I first began reading and studying *The Urantia Book,* I was concerned originally that I might find it difficult to wade through all of the verbiage. I thought that the book, based on what I knew of it, would offer such a stalwart resistance to my attempts to see through it that I would become exhausted in the attempt. What I found out was that nothing of the sort would occur. The reality is that *The Urantia Book* is a book that purports to tell the "real" story of God, the origins of this world and universe, and the truth behind the life, death, and resurrection of Jesus. In that, it fails.

The Urantia Book is not a book that is in any way, shape, or form compatible with the Bible or with Christianity. It is a book that is dressed up to appear as if it goes well beneath the surface of the Bible, unearthing jewels that the Bible somehow misses, yet it is clear that it is well off the mark entirely. It offers nothing that the New Age itself does not offer. It tries to vainly take the truth that the Bible provides and proceeds to attempt to turn that truth into a lie. It fails there as well, and it fails *obviously* for the judicious person.

Unfortunately, it will *not* fail for the person who wants to find something to *replace* the Bible. It will also not fail for the person who wants to find a god who can be buddied up to and simply followed, but not necessarily *worshiped*. We'll talk more about that in our next chapter when we delve into another New Age manifesto that seems to be gaining speed and momentum among adherents of the New Age.

The Urantia Book is nothing but a megalomaniac pretense. It is a *good* pretense, but nonetheless, it is a pretense. It overtly tries to be something that it is not and because of the lack of discernment among many today, a growing number of people will fall for it. They will read it and will do so gladly, because they will come to believe that *The Urantia Book* is the answer for which they have been searching throughout their entire life.

The truth of the matter is that aside from providing all of the alleged detail about Jesus' life, there is little here that stands out or separates itself from the volumes of works, tenets, and teachings already catalogued as New Age.

But we're not done yet. There are other books that we are going to take the time to look at to see if they in any way, shape, or form stand apart from the crowd, offering something that is not already found within the depths of the New Age in some form or another. So for that, please read on to find out if they fare any better.

THE BOOK OF LIFE

This particular book – allegedly transcribed by Archangel Michael – is one which cuts to the chase rather quickly. It's a no holds barred endeavor that attempts to slice and dice its way through the orthodoxy of Christianity specifically.

It begins with a gallop and ends with a minor warhead. As *The Urantia Book* tried delicately to persuade and convince, *The Book of Life* takes no real consideration of that, but deftly applies itself to carving holes in the truth of the Bible, the cross, and all things Christianity.

Why Should We Believe Them?

It's really a wake-up call for those who have already become disenchanted for one reason or another with Christianity and Christians. Because of the way *The Book of Life* is written, it will either be hailed as a masterpiece – a direct inroad to the truth that the Bible has allegedly tried to keep hidden – or it will be cast aside by those who need a softer approach, like *The Urantia Book* provides.

The Book of Life is not a long book and could easily be read by the average reader in an evening. The obvious problem with this book has to do with the way it presents things as fact in a fairly abrupt way. Unlike the way *The Urantia Book* presented the narrative, often doing so in a somewhat charming way that tended to draw the reader in, *The Book of Life* is almost completely devoid of any anesthesia, presenting information as if the reader is involved in a knife fight.

There is barely time to recover from one piece of information before another comes at you from another direction. As stated, while some individuals will marvel at the way this is done and will see this as a sign of its veracity, it is easy to see that too many people will find this style of writing off-putting.

For instance, on the book's cover, we read the following:

> "*Observe how the so-called Jews resurrected the devil, Dagon, as the one god. The letters in the name Dagon are rearranged to read, 'one god,' Monotheism. The 'a' and 'n' in Dagon spells, 'An" means 'one.' Then you have D-G-O remaing, which is rearranged as G-O-D, God. The devil was now the one god...the devil was then passed to you to worship as the one god. Be mindful then that all forms of worship are devil worship and are forbidden by Nature. The result if you worship anything, and do not stop while you are alive, is your*

> *death (sic). Eternity inside the sun, with the devil, the one god. So. Does your name appear in...THE BOOK OF LIFE?"*[38]

There is nothing in the book that explains how the individual came up with this information from a *rational* perspective. However, since the book *claims* to have been transcribed by Archangel Michael, that will be enough for some.

The interesting thing about many of these beings that exist outside our time or dimension is the fact that they seem to often act independently of any higher authority. Such is the case with this book and its alleged transcriber, Archangel Michael.

The substance of the book is essentially summed up with the short paragraph found on page 1: *"To eliminate disappointments, Nature allows us to choose either eternal life or eternal death. It is your free will choice. Nature now reveals that path you are on, so that you might choose wisely."*[39]

The Preface of the book introduces Archangel Michael to the reader: *"As the Archangel Michael, it is my pleasure, and my duty, to tell the truth. If I do not tell the truth, the title of Archangel is worthless. What you are about to read in the* Book of Life, *is the truth taken out of the Holy Bible. The Holy Bible can be interpreted in two ways. You can tell the lie that is written, or you can tell the truth that is written. It is my charge as The Archangel to reveal the truth that is written."*[40]

The book goes on to explain that apparently the first two people that Nature created were both male and female. In other words, both individuals were hermaphrodites, having sexual organs for both sexes. Also according to *The Book of Life*, there was a plot to eliminate her-

---

[38] *The Book of Life,* ("transcribed by Archangel Michael", 2008), front cover
[39] Ibid, 1
[40] Ibid, 3

maphrodites from existence. We also learn that the male gender of the human species was meant to be enslaved and tossed into death. This is an interesting statement considering the fact that the two original individuals allegedly had *both* sexes built into them.

"The purpose of this plot was to keep death in this world, and thereby rule the earth thru fear of death. The female however, could not have executed this plot without the help of her god, the devil. Of course, the hermaphrodite that the female would worship as god was A'belle. To accomplish her goal, the female gender of the human species, si willing to march head on into death, and drag every living human with her. The plot itself would be called, 'The tree of the knowledge of good and of evil,' also known as, the religion.

"In the Bible, 'The Tree of Knowledge of Good and Evil,' is symbolic for <u>religion</u>. Religions provide you with the knowledge of what is good and what is evil. Religions have always maintained the sole copyright to what you learned to be good and evil…The result of your involvement in religion is death. Nature has no part in death. Nature produces only life. Nature produced the tree of life, the truth. <u>Death is in the place where Nature confined the lord God, who hid the tree of life, so that the man, and all human life, would die. For this, Nature rightfully named the lord god, the devil</u>."[41] (emphasis in original)

Note that in this book, Archangel Michael first says that what he writes is based on the Holy Bible. However, he then introduces concepts that are not in the Bible at all. Also, apparently Nature is higher than the God of the Bible and this God is none other than the devil himself.

This book – *The Book of Life* – purports to be the final holy book, and it follows Revelation because it incorporates biblical subjects but

---

[41] *The Book of Life,* ("transcribed by Archangel Michael", 2008), 3-4

places them in a new book that is alleged to wrap things up. Throughout the book, the concept of destroying religion itself pops up frequently. In fact, the message is clear that because of religion, death continues.

Archangel Michael goes into some grammatical gymnastics by telling us where the word religion came from and what it means. *"The root word of the word religion is 'lig.' Lig means 'to Lie.' One need only remove the prefix 're,' and the suffix, 'ion,' from the word religion, to produce its root word, 'Lig.' Lig means, to lie. Therefore, the root of the word religion means, 'to lie.'*

"Now add the prefix, 're', which means 'anew,' to the root, 'to lie,' and you have, 'to lie anew.'

Including the suffix, 'ion,' which means, 'a process of being,' and you have, <u>'a process to lie anew.'</u> That is the natural meaning of the world religion, 'a process to lie anew.' <u>All religion</u>.

"If the root of the tree is a lie, is not the fruit of the tree a lie?"[42]

We further learn that the book of Genesis is not the book that literally recorded the beginnings. It is actually a book of *genes*. In essence then, the book of Genesis is a book about who has which genes and why.

The book also tells us that those who follow Jesus actually follow Him to death and hell. Reading through *The Book of Life* is at once confusing and seems to have been written by someone who has a very limited understand of the English language. Sentences are short, often repeated, and seemingly devoid of any type of factual evidence for the statements made.

---

[42] *The Book of Life,* ("transcribed by Archangel Michael", 2008), 11

Why Should We Believe Them?

Too often, the statements that are presented are done in such a way (like *The Urantia Book*) that simply presents the information. Great emphasis is placed on what the Bible does *not* say, for instance, as opposed to what it *does* say. Those apparent silences of the biblical record provide great fodder for this work.

As was expected, the God of the Bible is a god who tries to pull one over on humanity, and for the most part succeeds. He allegedly hid the Tree of Life from the man/woman named A'dam, but not from Eve. The assumptions continually made in *The Book of Life* are far-fetched at best, including the idea that both A'dam and Eve were women and because of that could not have produced either Cain or Abel.

I laughed a bit when I read that though we learned over time that both Adam and Eve ate the apple, there is no mention of apple in the Bible. To that, it can be responded that the idea that the apple was the fruit was probably the result of some 5th Avenue marketing company, because the fruit mentioned in the Bible is not specifically named. We have no idea what the actual fruit was that both Adam and Eve ate. However, Archangel Michael uses that in an attempt to prove that this makes the Bible false.

Other concepts come to the fore, like the idea that it is not God who is in charge, but Nature. Nature controls everything. In essence, the major point of *The Book of Life* is that Nature is in control and simply presents you with a choice. That choice is eternal life or eternal death. Death means that you go inside the sun to burn forever.

Eternal life is something that we must choose, and that is extremely easy once we understand the principle involved. To gain eternal life, according to Archangel Michael, we must simply decide to never worship *anything*, ever. Once we start to worship something, we become slaves to that thing. It becomes our god and we willingly place ourselves under its headship. Once we do this, we begin the process of dying.

We learn about the devil and about the fact that he apparently is represented by a horned hat, similar to the one the Pontiff of the Roman Catholic Church wears. We are born free, but the devil (who happens to be a woman) wants to take that freedom from each of us and does so through our involvement in religion.

It also comes as no surprise that Lucifer – as far as *The Book of Life* is concerned – is the truth: Light. In other words, the tables were turned by Jesus. He took what belonged to Lucifer and through the religious orders turned Lucifer into the devil. So whatever you have heard or learned about the God of the Bible is false. It is Lucifer that is the true god and guide.

Archangel Michael reveals to us that there is no physical place called heaven, as it was something that was never created. The Garden of Eden was originally the Garden of Need because the devil simply switched the letters around from Eden to get Need.

It is interesting (but again, not surprising) that according to Archangel Michael Jews are actually devils. Beyond this, other "jewels" stand out in this book; for instance, incest between parents and child is part of the natural aspect of life. It is natural, therefore there is nothing wrong with it. Of course, religion came in to tell people that there is something wrong with it, but since religion is bad and wants to enslave, then it should be avoided.

Moreover, Moses never really existed and neither did Jesus. It was all a lie, created by the religious establishment to shut down our own sovereign choice to gain eternal life.

The Book of Life closes with the following words called The Path:

"If you worship anything, you have now been found wanting. If you have passed the tree of the knowledge of good and of evil, religion, to a child, you have now been found wanting.

"If you do not give each human the profits of their labor, you have now been found wanting. If you have not enjoyed incest, in truth and in love, you have now been found wanting.

"If you believe that any drug nature has created is bad, you have now been found wanting.

"The wages of sin was never death. There never was any sin.

"The wages of living unnatural is death, eternity inside the sun."[43]

What is there to say about a book such as this? It is devoid of any real redeeming value and I find it difficult to believe that anyone would take it seriously.

At the same time, we have had people who have banded together to kill themselves as Halle Bop passed over so that they could hitch a ride on the UFO that was apparently flying behind it, just out of sight.

We have had thousands of people die in cults like those led by Jim Jones.

We have seen the after effects of false prophets, religious leaders who are in it for the money only, and a variety of scams that have infiltrated the church and people's lives.

People today have little to no discernment and it is tragic. The individual who put this book together likely believes that the 100 pages of it contain truth heretofore unrecognized or revealed. There is not one modicum of evidence to support the claims of Archangel Michael,

---

[43] *The Book of Life* ("transcribed by Archangel Michael", 2008), 100

and yet it is clear that there will be some who will read this and breathe a sigh of relief.

They will become excited in the fact that they now have permission to use any drug they want, have incest to their heart's content, and reject the concept of sin that permeates the Bible.

In essence, *The Book of Life* takes everything previously understood from the biblical record and turns it on its head. What I find most interesting in all of this is the fact that the Michael from the Bible (of whom the transcriber of *The Book of Life* claims to be) rarely spoke, and it is clear that he only did what the Lord commanded.

The Archangel Michael connected with *The Book of Life* has his own opinions, his own interpretation of Scripture, and in the end calls the Bible a lie. Deciding whom to believe seems to be a no-brainer.

I would avoid this book and its teachings unless you simply want a good laugh or you have absolutely nothing better to do. It is a very coarse, uneven, and juvenile attempt to undermine the Bible and God, and the message contains aspects of New Age "theology" by elevating Satan (Lucifer) and lowering Jesus.

13

THE MESSAGE OF UFOS

UFOs have been making headlines for decades, but with the onset of Y2K and beyond, it seems that they have been throwing caution to the wind. In fact, even *before* the year 2000, UFOs had been reportedly seen en masse in various places throughout the world routinely. Mexico has had plenty of sightings as has Israel, parts of Russia, the UK and elsewhere.

It is as if people have finally gotten past the point of believing that aliens are not real or wish to harm us. There are groups of people as well as individuals who have been searching for that alien message from the great beyond for decades. It seems that now, the time is right and aliens have begun taking greater steps to reveal themselves to the world.

But what is their message? Is it something that we can benefit from? I find it interesting that nearly without fail, the messages that are received from alleged aliens are little more than religious Bible studies or sermons. That seems odd considering that these beings are supposed to be far more advanced than the rest of us on earth.

I mean, after all, their ships can move from one place to another in virtually the blink of an eye. That type of propulsion system is without doubt something this earth could benefit from having. To date, they have not shared their secrets. While some might argue that with that information, we could blow the earth up quicker, the real reasons may be something else entirely.

But let's set aside the interest in their source of propulsion and deal with something much more pragmatic. How about the issue of diseases? As we know, this world's society is reeling from one major fatal disease after another. Whether it's AIDS, cancers, or something else entirely, there are many things that are killing people at unprecedented rates and scientists seem no closer to real cures today than they were yesterday. Yes, there is some promising research that has narrowed things down and because of that we are a bit closer to a cure, but there is still a long way to go.

So, why aren't these super-intelligent beings providing us with information that could cure some of these diseases? Even a cure for the common cold would be more than welcome.

Instead, we learn from these beings all we wanted to know (and more) about religion at its finest (according to them). We have spent a good portion of this book delving into the depths of *The Urantia*

Book and other works. As is so often the case, regardless of how the information in these books is put forth, what it all boils down to is that the Bible is wrong and the real answer is found in this latest book. Why are these beings so concerned about whether or not we understand religion and religious concepts "correctly"? It really doesn't add up…unless, of course, they are here to pull the wool over our eyes and distract us from ascertaining the truth.

In the book *UFOS and the Extraterrestrial Message*, we learn a good deal of things…about *religion*. Gee, what a surprise. Even in the book's Introduction, we immediately see where the book is headed. Talk of the Star of Bethlehem surfaces, and this is connected to an Englishman roughly 2,000 years after the event.

It seems that this man (along with many others) wanted to find out more about that particular star. What was it, a plain star, a meteor, or something else?

As our English friend sat overlooking the ocean "*in a yogic posture, praying for peace in the world,*"[44] he saw "*a bright blue sphere skipping across the night sky. It stopped dead in its tracks over the sea before him and hovered. He continued to pray.*"[45]

According to the narrative, a being appeared to him that appeared to be connected to the blue sphere. He surmised that it was "*the same being the wise men had seen so long ago, standing just a few years away from him, but this time not in swaddling clothes. He stood tall, radiant, and dressed from the shoulders to the ground in a robe that seemed to glow with a bluish-white incandescence. The Master Jesus had come to Holdstone Down, near Combe Martin in Devon, England, to charge it with spiritual power through the channel he had chosen*

---

[44] Richard Lawrence *UFOs and the Extraterrestrial Message* (CICO Books, 2010), 2
[45] Ibid, 2

*for this task, the yoga master Dr. George King."*⁴⁶ I'm assuming the man believed this to be Jesus because he probably looked like many of the pictures and paintings of Him we have seen for generations. However, is that enough proof?

Apparently, Jesus hung out for a short period of time and then vanished. Here is how it happened. *"[Jesus] fixed me with a penetrating but kindly gaze for a moment, then a wide beam of green light sprang out of a faintly luminous shape hovering above the ground, about thirty yards away. The Master Jesus moved a few steps to one side, into this beam – and was gone...*

*"High up in the heavens I saw two bluish spheres of light, like two bright unblinking stars. They were joined by a third which came upwards to meet them. Then these three spacecraft traveled quickly across the skies to disappear over the western horizon. I knew that He had returned to the cosmos and my mission was completed."*⁴⁷

So apparently, the individual who was meditating using the "Dr. George King" channel, managed to bring Jesus back to earth so that He could release power to that area of the world. When He had completed His mission, He left, literally being beamed up to a waiting spacecraft.

This event is still marked and commemorated by people in that area of the world, who offer prayers of thanks to these beings from other worlds. In fact, roughly five decades later, as the event was being remembered by the faithful, *"one of the biggest spates of UFO sightings occurred in various parts of the British Isles, as reported in the national press for several days."*⁴⁸

---

[46] Richard Lawrence *UFOs and the Extraterrestrial Message* (CICO Books, 2010), 2
[47] Ibid, 2-3
[48] Ibid, 3

Of course, these events are deemed *good* by those who are looking for them for one simple reason: *personal experience.*

Because of the way our world is moving, with all of its death, disease, violence, war, and everything else that is considered to be negative, more and more people are coming round to believe that a planetary divine intervention is necessary in order to save not only the planet, but the people who live here.

This is all well and good, but the problems of this world cannot be solved by the beings from other dimensions that have created those problems to exist in the first place. Satan has been a murderer from the beginning, prompting Cain to kill his brother Abel, and why? He did it because he (Cain) was jealous of Abel's proper sacrifice. Satan has always been a liar, telling his first lie to humans with Eve. He continues to lie to this day.

We have finally reached a point in our societal growth where technology is moving faster than we are moving. This has created an untenable situation where it has become impossible to keep up with how fast it moves. We try. We no sooner purchase the latest cell phone or computer than we learn that within three to six months something else comes along to replace it, making ours outmoded.

Computers go faster. Access to and on the Internet is faster. Our cell phones go further to gain a signal. Our life is filled with contrivances that are supposed to make our life easier, but in truth, I'm not sure that's the case.

We have become a world that is addicted to technology and with the possible exception of North Korea, it might be impossible for us to get along without our technology because of our growing dependence upon it.

Years ago, I would go to the bank and make a deposit or withdrawal and the teller would mark my physical bank book. There were no such things as debit cards or electronic banking. It simply did not exist.

Now, I can do my banking online if I choose to do so. I have a debit card that allows me to purchase anything I want and I can take cash out of my account from just about anywhere.

The world has gone digital and it shows. Even in movies, the reality that is now created by digital special effects far surpasses anything that physical special effects were capable of creating. Video games are also a case in point. The digital effects and rotoscoping that is used today to create realistic gaming experiences goes well beyond anything that has come before it.

We expect our world to be able to do what we see in movies. We actually expect it, and so for us UFOs and aliens are simply part of that picture. It is this growth of technology that has literally catapulted us into the future, even before we have actually arrived there. We think it, therefore we believe it can be accomplished, and we're not that far off.

The movie "Tron: Legacy" recently released by Disney is a sequel to the original movie shot years ago. I will admit that I never saw the first "Tron," but when this second one came out I decided to check it out with my son because of the effects. I really did not know what the story was all about except that the main character – played by Jeff Bridges – was able to go *inside* the grid – inside the computer.

The movie's effects were startlingly good. It is easy to get lost in a movie like this, thinking that the things the characters in the movie were capable of are not that far off for us.

After watching this latest "Tron," I decided to watch the original. It was interesting, but so ancient compared with the new version, it was difficult to take it seriously. I tried to keep putting myself back into the 70s, realizing that for that time period, even this movie was a bit ahead of its time. The truth of the matter, though, is that within a little over thirty years the technology between the two movies was astronomically different, with the second being far superior.

Of course, with the second movie, the New Age mantras and tenets ran throughout. It was so obvious that it was a bit pitiful, yet I also knew that many would be drawn into that thinking because they lean toward it anyway.

Jeff Bridges' character constantly spoke of his "zen" and things called ISOs, which were a brand new form of the current program and something that the program did not necessarily envision. In my view, this is a nod to evolution. These ISOs could replicate and even repair themselves. The arch enemy of the film – Clu – had them destroyed because he saw them as not being perfect since they were not part of the original plan. Clu failed to destroy all of them, and the last remaining ISO – Chorra – teamed with Jeff Bridges' character and his son to overthrow Clu.

More movies today carry the theme that this world needs something far greater in order for it to survive. The book *UFOs and the Extraterrestrial Message* says as much. *"If ever we needed the help of the gods, the Cosmic Masters, call them what you will, it is surely now. After all, we are facing dire warnings on the ecological front; we have the capacity to destroy ourselves for the first time in this civilization; mass overpopulation is a problem; as many conflicts as ever are raging, with far more deadly weapons to carry them out; and we are up against a new kind of terrorism, not to mention poverty on a gigantic scale.* **Why should we be scouring old records** *for evidence of miraculous happenings, of intervention from above, or* **escaping into the world of**

***fiction** to grapple with extraordinary events, when by any reckoning they should be happening now?"*[49] (emphasis added)

Note how the author – Richard Lawrence – dissuades people from looking backwards by stating that we should not be wasting our time looking at "old records," which I take to mean the Bible and possibly other books of antiquity. We should let go of those things because they are in the past and, according to Lawrence, have no ability to help us in the present.

Because of this mentality, more and more people are opening themselves up to these alien beings, believing that they are altruistic, benign, kind, and simply want to help. The beings themselves offer a sort of proof of this by the very fact that they have remained hidden for so long. They haven't wanted to deliberately scare people with their presence, so they wait until the time is right to reveal themselves.

In the meantime, they work through specific individuals who have believed them and opened themselves up to them. It is through these people that they speak to the rest of humanity because these people believe that these beings have a plan for our world and that plan needs to be placed out in the open. More than that, it needs to be explored, honored, and especially *received* and accepted. Lawrence himself states that his book is meant to "*deal with the all-important issue of their plan for our world.*"[50]

The problem, of course – though not stated by Lawrence – is that there is no way to fully and accurately determine whether or not the beings that come to us in the form of messengers of light or something similar are being up front with us. Lawrence believes he has an

---

[49] Richard Lawrence *UFOs and the Extraterrestrial Message* (CICO Books, 2010), 4
[50] Ibid, 7

answer to that potential problem. *"Subjective, as well as objective experience is of vital importance as a means of determining the truth. Some people will accept objective evidence only, and they will find that here, but in the final analysis, we often accept what we know at an intuitive level just as much, if not more, than something that has been demonstrated to us through rational deduction and intellectual argument. The big decisions we take in our personal lives are a result of our innermost feelings – we don't choose our life partner because we have been convinced to do so in a debating forum but because we know we love them."*[51]

This is exactly what I spoke of at the beginning of this book. Lawrence is wrong. Most of the decisions we make in our life that have a profound effect on us (or can) are done by comparing and contrasting. We weigh the good with the bad, or the positive with the negative.

Choosing a college or job or even a career path is not something people do lightly. With respect to marrying a person, yes, often our emotions overrule our intellect. That can be a good thing, but with the divorce rate as high as it currently is, it may not be a good thing. While feelings start us off toward our future mate, feelings also often push us away because we see love as purely a feeling, and since feelings can come and go, there is no guarantee that the feeling of love will remain.

I am glad that God's love for me does not rely on His feeling for me. I'm glad instead it relies on the fact of His nature and is also based on a specific decision by Him to love me. It was that love that prompted Him to follow through with the plan of salvation in order that I might know Him and be saved by Him. His love followed through so that I

---

[51] Richard Lawrence *UFOs and the Extraterrestrial Message* (CICO Books, 2010), 8

can have eternal life, and when I leave this planet I will have eternal life in all its fullness, something that I cannot now have because I have a corrupted (dying) body that contains the sin nature.

Throughout *UFOs and the Extraterrestrial Message*, Lawrence shares with us the research he has done into this field of UFOlogy. He shares with us many instances of people who allegedly made contact with beings from other worlds and other dimensions.

He speaks a good deal about Dr. George King, and according to Lawrence, in 1954 while alone in his apartment King heard a loud voice say to him, "*Prepare yourself! You are to become the voice of Interplanetary Parliament.*"[52] Dr. King went on to form the "Atherius Society" and also published "Cosmic Voice." Admittedly, he channeled many messages from beyond this world and dimension.

Due to his connections with ascended masters, he began two projects that he believed would help mankind evolve: *Operation Sunbeam* and *Operation Prayer Power*.

Operation Prayer Power seeks to gather and then direct energy through a type of prayer. One might wonder how this could be used for humanity's good. "*The spiritual energy of prayer is one of the greatest healing forces available to mankind. It can be used to heal individuals and groups alike. It is truly the power of Love in action. Prayer has been taught throughout the ages, and it forms an essential part of all major religions. Millions of people throughout the world regularly use this form of energy and help the world more than they may realize. When an earthquake or other such catastrophe occurs on earth, millions of spiritually minded people send their prayers to help those in need. This is like gentle rain falling upon an uncontrolled fire. The more who join in prayer, the harder the rain falls. Imagine if one could har-*

---

[52] Richard Lawrence *UFOs and the Extraterrestrial Message* (CICO Books, 2010), 34

ness the rain, collect it together and pour it in a flowing stream onto such a raging fire of suffering. The effects would be multiplied exponentially. Dr. King's mission Operation Prayer Power does just this."[53]

According to King, Jesus taught him that *"Man dwelleth in a world of selfishness – God dwelleth in a world of selfless expansion. Bridge this gap – and be a GOD."*[54] So King set off to teach the world about this selfless expansion and Operation Prayer Power was designed to do just that – teach people to be selfless by directing their energies to those in need throughout the globe.

In Operation Sunbeam, people take the energy that exists and instead of directing it toward humanity, they direct it toward Mother Earth. This allows Mother Earth to heal and even evolve to her next level of planetary movement.

Shortly after Dr. King heard the voice that was to tell him he would become the voice of Interplanetary Parliament, he was visited by a yogi from India. Allegedly, this yogi walked right through a closed and locked door to appear right before King. The Swami explained and taught King the virtues and values he needed for his mission, then just as he appeared, he left.

Of course, people will accept this as truth because it is very reminiscent of Jesus and how He moved about society following His resurrection. We are told that He walked through walls, yet was able to eat food (cf. Matthew 28:1-20; Mark 16:1-20; Luke 24:1-49; John 20:1-21:25). To us, these are feats of magic, yet to Jesus, it was the norm for Him in His resurrected, glorified body. Those who are familiar with these stories, yet are not Christian, will find a connection

---

[53] http://www.aetherius.org/index.cfm?app=content&SectionID=80&PageID=55 (accessed 5/23/11)
[54] http://www.aetherius.org/index.cfm?app=content&SectionID=36 (accessed 5/23/11)

between the incidents in Jesus' life and that one here in the life of Dr. George King.

Lawrence also spends a good amount of time highlighting many supposed sightings that have also allegedly been covered up over past decades. Of course, we know that governments routinely tell the public nothing about UFOs. This leaves people to imagine what they will, and most who believe in UFOs believe that the government has far more information than they are willing to let on.

We also know from recent Wikileaked documents that UFOs have been part of a loose-knit conspiracy cover-up. The biggest reason that the governments use for not releasing any information is that either 1) the information does not exist, or 2) the information does not exist and releasing certain documents would risk national security.

Because of this, many are left in the dark to simply wonder about things. The problem is that we have a greater number of people than ever coming forward with their claims, and the continued denial by various governments simply serves to feed the fires of conspiracy.

I have spent time in previous books cataloguing various first-person tales of alleged alien contact. Lawrence offers more of the same; however, Lawrence is not a skeptic. He firmly believes that the beings and craft people are claiming to see are true, for the most part.

Lawrence believes that these entities are who they say they are and should be accepted as they present themselves. Other writers – Christians – like L. A. Marzulli, Chuck Missler, this author, and others, arrive at the biblical conclusion that these beings are nothing but imposters, demons masquerading as intelligent ascended masters, or aliens.

Lawrence provides many accounts of alleged contact with these aliens and descriptions range from short beings to tall ones, beings with blonde hair to no hair. The craft themselves have been described as cigar-shaped to round to triangular. They have dark eyes to pink-colored eyes. Some of them say nothing, while others telepathically speak. It is a wide-open area that does not seem to have any one source or description.

What it looks like is that not all aliens are of the same culture group. They are far more varied than people gave them credit for being decades ago. However, no matter which culture group the aliens seem to be from, once again, the message is much the same.

This tends to work in the aliens' favor because people then say that since the same essential message comes from a variety of aliens and their own culture groups, how can the message be wrong? However, wouldn't different culture groups have different messages? That is certainly true of the earth's culture groups. No two cultures seem to have the same beliefs about anything.

Of course, Lawrence also reaches way back into human history and tends to at least try to make the connection between ancient aliens and religion. The Bible is not overlooked here either, and one of the favorite sections of the Bible that UFOlogists often turn is the book of Ezekiel or 2 Kings. There, the description of God's glory as seen in the first few chapters is likened to UFOs, much the way the book *Chariots of the Gods* does.

Lawrence also deals with the concept of living within a multi-dimensional universe. Of late, more UFOlogists are coming to believe that aliens are not necessarily from other worlds per se, but from other dimensions. These dimensions in nearly all cases butt up against ours, and because of the technology available to the aliens, they are able to transverse the dimensions without a problem, something human beings cannot do in our present state.

Apparently, according to Dr. George King, there is a Primary Terrestrial Mental Channel, through which the Cosmis Masters are able to connect with humanity. It is also through this channel that energy can be collected and directed toward others in need, or to the earth itself during terrible times.

Such was the case regarding Chernobyl and the nuclear reactor situation. According to Lawrence, Dr. King's organization had learned of the event within days and had begun to direct necessary healing energy toward the earth then.

Some sixteen years later, Russia released its own citing how the explosion could have been far worse except for the help from a UFO, which many had seen hovering above the reactor site for hours right after the explosion. This was actually right in the official report, according to Lawrence.

So time after time, we hear of these events that are causing people to lower their guard. I mean, let's face it, if UFOs are here to help, it certainly seems as though that's what they have been doing. They have been sending us messages that are designed to help us gather ourselves, our energy, and our resolve, and corporately move society and the earth itself toward the next spiritual plane.

If that's the case, what can be so bad or harmful about alien contacts that have allegedly been made? A couple of things. Obviously, if aliens are correct, then Christianity is wrong. The two are incompatible. On the other hand, if Christianity is correct, then something strange is going on in the area of aliens and Alienology.

I do not doubt that "aliens" of a sort have made contact with society. I further do not doubt that specific individuals have been chosen by aliens to act as mouthpieces for the aliens. Normally, these people seem to have been chosen because either they were already well involved in areas of New Age through meditation, mantras, and believing in the tenets of the New Age, or they were completely open to it and moving in that direction already.

Extremely rare is the case of an authentic Christian becoming involved in the area of aliens or ascended masters. In those cases, when it does happen it seems that the aliens have been immediately stopped when the person began praying to Jesus. Cases such as these have been written about in L.A. Marzulli's books.

If you remove Christianity from the picture completely, you are left with a variety of religions that simply cater to the wants of humanity. Like Adam and Eve, who believed the false claims of the Tempter, aliens come with similar messages. These messages seem to be designed to lower our resistance.

Isn't it the same way a superior con artist works? They try to trap their mark through a variety of means. First, it is extremely helpful and important that the con artist knows as much about their subject as possible. It would not do to know little to nothing about the person, depending upon the con itself.

Some cons are more appropriate for groups of people because in general, people in groups can often be gullible. Other cons are directed at specific people, and because of that require a good deal of insider knowledge in order for the con to work.

Demons live in the spiritual realm. Accordingly, and as the Bible attests, these beings can come in and out of our physical realm at will. They can also physically possess people too, based on a variety of things.

Think about the fact that these beings that exist normally in other dimensions, but are able to interact with us in our dimensions, are generally invisible to us. This does not mean they do not exist. It simply means that we cannot see them. In other words, we are at *their* mercy. We will only see them or hear from them if they want that to happen.

Consider also the fact that many people have been diligently searching for any sign of cosmic intelligent life and they have been doing so for decades (in my lifetime, for instance). As more people open themselves up to these beings, the greater their chance of being contacted by one. Why is that?

It exists because these beings can see our every move. They know what we eat, when we sleep, what we do for fun, and what our interests are in life. They see that many people have become interested in intelligent life from beyond our world. Movies have played a large part in creating this interest, but whatever the source, they know who is and who is not interested.

They also know who is susceptible to their suggestions and they know who really, *really* wants to make contact with them. It is a no-brainer to them, so they simply reveal what they want to reveal to their "mark" because they know that person is not only open to it, but susceptible to the suggestions and teachings that stem from any contact that is made.

You see, there is a plethora of people today who truly *want* to believe that aliens do exist. Because of this, these people are on the search, and they simply want to have confirmation of what they already *believe*. For them, it is not that they need to be convinced of anything; it is the desire to experience what they believe to be fact. When it does happen, they believe it because of their mindset that tells them it is real, above board, and absolutely authentic.

Years ago, I used to watch the TV show *Mission Impossible*. It was a great show because the IMF people would go through this elaborate scheme to gain the upper hand over a certain individual in order to have that person give them the information they were looking for or do what they needed him/her to do. Because of that the con was often in-depth and very detailed, but it always worked because though there might have been some resistance initially, the mark normally gave in and believed that everything they were experiencing was totally on the up and up, only to discover later that it was not.

This is exactly the way I believe it to be with beings from the spiritual realm, beings referred to as aliens or ascended masters. In one way or another, they always say what the mark wants to hear. The Bible is not real, or it is real, but severely misinterpreted. Jesus did not exist, or He did exist, but not as we normally think of Him.

Sin does not exist, or sin is merely our failure to love one another more completely. Hell does not exist physically, because it's simply a frame of mind. Eternal life has already been given. It is each individual's job to actualize it within us.

There is never an alien who tells us that the Bible is correct, that God the Son is Jesus and the plan of redemption is just that, God's plan to save humanity. That never happens. Beyond that, we are never given any information by these aliens that help us eradicate suffering, hunger, or war. It does not come out of their mouth to our brains. They aren't even willing to share some of their technological advances with us.

So what gives? What is the scoop on all of this? Obviously, you'll decide for yourself what the scoop is, but before you read my full opinion on the matter, let's move to our next chapter and deal with Scientology. Is it a religion, an ideology, or one huge con?

SCIENTOLOGY & ALIENS

L Ron Hubbard has always been an interesting figure. In many ways, he was larger than life. He was an author of numerous Sci-Fi related books and founder of an ideology known as *Scientology*. Of course, those connected to Scientology claim that it is a religion, but they've had their share of legal problems with organizations like the Internal Revenue Service over just such an issue. The Food and Drug Administration (FDA) also got involved because of the use of what Scientology refers to as E-meters. The E-meters were confiscated from Scientology headquarters and the organization was only permitted to continue using them after labeling them conspicuously with the statement that they were a religious artifact. Scientologists insist that the E-meter, when used by trained officials during auditing sessions, will detect when a person is relieved from past traumas.

Auditing is a term that essentially means the individual goes back into their past through counseling to remember painful or even traumatic events that have occurred in their life. Once they remember them, they work to become free of their debilitating effects. This is how one grows through the system that has been developed within Scientology. *Dianetics* is another well-known term. The process of Dianetics relies fully on auditing. So, auditing is built into Dianetics.

The Scientology organization has been dogged by controversy and at one time it was outlawed in Australia, though they later changed their mind. Other countries like Canada and Wales refused to register the organization as a religion.[55]

This particular book – *What is Scientology?* – attempts to trace things back throughout the ages to show that many religions have come under scrutiny and dispute. This in and of itself does not mean that those religions are not legitimate. It simply means that the way people *view* them can mean one thing at one point in time and something else at another point in time.

The book then spends some time providing a biography of L. Ron Hubbard's life and shows him as being meritorious as well as a world traveler. It was this that allowed him to gain insight into the many

---

[55] http://en.wikipedia.org/wiki/Scientology#Dispute_of_religion_status (accessed 5/23/11)

religions of the world. To read this part of the book, one would believe that Hubbard was the modern day Ghandi who went about helping people wherever he found himself. A book can be printed to say anything. What is of more importance is what society often says about a person or an organization.

"BBC journalist Stewart Lamont, in research for his book, Religion Inc., obtained court documents in the case revealing that Justice Latey of the High Court of London called Scientology a 'cult,' and wrote in the judgment, 'Scientology is both immoral and socially obnoxious.... It is corrupt, sinister, and dangerous' (p. 149)."[56]

Many believe that Hubbard was thoroughly involved in the occult. *"Jon Atack, a former Scientologist and highly repected [sic] biographer of Hubbard and Scientology, has collected probably the most extensive research archives on Scientology. Atack writes, 'It is impossible to arrive at an understanding of Scientology without taking into account its creator's extensive involvement with magic' (FactNet Report, "Hubbard and the Occult" p. 2).*

"Atack states that when one examines Hubbard's private letters and papers which were revealed in the Church of Scientology vs. Armstrong trial, and compares the teachings of Scientology with those of the infamous occultist Aleister Crowley, the connection is inescapable (Ibid.).

"Hubbard was clearly involved in the occult. In 1945, L. Ron Hubbard met Jack Parsons, who was a renowned scientist, protégé of occultist Aleister Crowley, and a member of the notorious Ordo Templi Orientis (O.T.O.), an international organization founded by Crowley to practice sexual black magic."[57]

---

[56] http://www.watchman.org/sci/hubmagk2.htm (accessed 5/23/11)
[57] Ibid

"Hubbard was clearly involved in the occult. In 1945, L. Ron Hubbard met Jack Parsons, who was a renowned scientist, protégé of occultist Aleister Crowley, and a member of the notorious Ordo Templi Orientis (O.T.O.), an international organization founded by Crowley to practice sexual black magic.

"Parsons had Hubbard move onto the property of Parsons' Pasadena, California, home. It was there that Hubbard began to practice the occult and sexual magic. Parsons' mistress, Sara Northrup, left him for Hubbard and later became Hubbard's second wife, even before Hubbard had divorced his first wife (The Los Angeles Times, June 24, 1990, p. A37)."[58]

Of course, there are many other incidents of Hubbard's alleged involvement with the occult and things satanic. This would explain why many of the teachings within Scientology compare so favorably with other aspects of the New Age movement.

Near to the central teachings of Scientology is the idea that man is composed of three parts: *mind, thetan, and body.* The Thetan represents the spiritual mind. Beyond this, there are eight dynamics within the system of Scientology:

1. **Self**: *The effort to survive as an individual.*
2. **Creativity**: *Making things for the future.*
3. **Group Survival**: *Effort to survive in a group or through a group.*
4. **Species**: *The urge to survive as part of mankind and through all of mankind.*
5. **Life Forms**: *The urge to survive as life forms and with the help of other life forms.*

---

[58] http://www.watchman.org/sci/hubmagk2.htm (accessed 5/23/11)

6. **Physical Universe**: *Made up of four components. These are matter, energy, space and time.*
7. **Spiritual**: *The urge to survive as spiritual beings or the urge for life itself to survive.*
8. **Infinity**: *The urge toward existence as INFINITY. [This] is also called GOD.*

As indicated, Scientologists believe that man is composed of three parts: *mind, thetan,* and *body*. The thetan actually connects with *aliens*. In L. Ron Hubbard's beliefs, *thetans* were originally aliens, and many were attacked and killed by an evil alien ruler named *Xenu*. Surviving thetans then attached themselves to human beings.

However, the job of human beings is literally to rid ourselves of these leechy thetans. This is where *auditing* comes in because it requires the use of auditing (and the aforementioned *e-meter*) to know when a person is *clear* of the thetan connection.

Auditing is not cheap. Obviously, the rich and famous are able to pay for these sessions (ranging into the thousands of dollars per session), but the poor not so much. In fact, the lower echelon of believers within Scientology is not aware of the thetan/Xenu connection, and if asked about it, would normally deny it truthfully, since they do not know of it. Only those who can pay for the sessions learn of this.

As many know, adherents within Scientology refuse psychiatric help and/or medication as Scientology is adamantly opposed to it and denies that there is anything like what people refer to as a chemical imbalance in the brain. Because of this, Scientology has come under fire for keeping medication from its members, and some members have died because of it.

Because of Hubbard's penchant for Sci-Fi, either he made the story up completely, or believed that he came to the knowledge of this information through a variety of ways. However, once again, we have a group that believes that aliens have exercised some control over this planet and the people on it.

Because of that, it is difficult to prove or disprove, and like just about everything else in the alien arena, it is left up to the individual to decide for themselves.

Certainly, in some ways, much of what Hubbard has published appears to lean solely toward the area of science fiction, without any basis in fact. Because the entire area of aliens is so unknown and based on people's *experiences,* it is almost impossible to disprove or verify.

When all is said and done, Scientology seems to be made up of a mixture of science fiction and gobbledy-gook in a not-so-grand form. Nonetheless, it has garnered the attention of people all over the world.

While Scientology leaders will tell us that they are the fastest growing religion, the facts tend to dispute that. Had Scientology simply been part of the overall New Age movement, it may have had a greater chance of success. However, it is clear from the study of Hubbard's own life that his plan may have been to create something new solely for the sake of money.

In the end, Scientology has taken its cue from a number of sources to create something that is extremely secretive (the higher up one goes) and costs a great deal of money to train through. That alone tends to sidetrack their claim that they are a religion. They are more likely a secret organization that ultimately caters to the rich, because it is the rich that can afford to pay the kind of money required to gain in the inside knowledge about Scientology.

A COURSE IN MIRACLES

A *Course in Miracles* is a well-known text connected with Helen Schucman. Schucman, with the help of William Thetford, composed the book based on what she heard within her, something she called her "inner voice." She believed the inner voice was the voice of Jesus.

Essentially, *A Course in Miracles* emphasizes the fact that miracles exist. In fact, the basic line of thinking here is that if miracles do *not* happen, then something is wrong, because miracles are supposed to be a natural part of each person's life.

Because there is a good deal of Christian-sounding terminology within *Course*, it tends to make the uninitiated believe that it is a Christian work and that it agrees with what the Bible teaches. This is far from the truth and the work has come under a great deal of criticism for this.

The book teaches that people should be involved in performing miracles every day. Miracles are simply a matter of fact, according to *Course*, as opposed to something out of the ordinary.

The actual text for *A Course in Miracles* contains 31 chapters, and through it we learn just exactly what *Course* teaches. If the reader is not careful, they will take what is stated in *Course* as biblically correct and fully legitimate. However, care must be utilized here because of the distraction that is created by the fact that *Course* constantly refers to God, Jesus, the Holy Spirit, and the Bible.

In chapter two, under the title *The Separation and the Atonement*, we read these words that describe for us the Garden of Eden and its original purpose:

"The Garden of Eden, or the pre-separation condition, was a state of mind in which nothing was needed. When Adam listened to the 'lies of the serpent,' all he heard was untruth. You do not have to continue to believe what is not true unless you choose to do so. All that can literally disappear in the twinkling of an eye because it is merely a misperception. What is seen in the dreams seems to be very real. Yet the Bible says that a deep sleep feel upon Adam, and nowhere is there reference to his waking up. The world has not yet experienced any comprehensive reawakening or rebirth. Such a rebirth is impossible as long as you continue to project or miscreate. It still remains within you, however, to extend as God extended His Spirit to you. In reality this is your only

choice, because your free will has given you for your joy in creating the perfect."[59]

Here we learn that the Garden of Eden – according to *Course* – was a state of mind. We also learn that Adam was put into a deep sleep from which he allegedly never woke. While *Course* is literalistically correct in stating that he never woke up (according to the Bible), it is clearly inferred from Scripture.

The reason God put Adam to sleep (cf. Genesis 2) was for the sole purpose of taking one of Adam's ribs in order to make Eve. Once God completed this surgery, Eve was there. It is similar to reading a story about a man who goes into a grocery store empty-handed. When he comes out, he has a bag. The story does not tell us what is in the bag nor does it state that he actually bought the items. We rightly infer, though, that he *did* buy specific items and they are now contained in the bag he carries.

If the author of the story wanted us to know that the man did *not* buy anything, but merely found a bag, opened it and carried it like there were items in it, it is reasonable to conclude that the author of said story would tell us that. The fact that he/she allows the reader to believe that the man purchased specific items and went to the cashier and paid for them would be disingenuous if this did not actually happen. That author would know (or should know) that everyone reading the story would naturally assume that the man went to the store empty-handed, bought specific items at the cash register, put the items in the bag, and then left with the bag of items.

In the same way, the implicit nature of the Creation story indicates to us that of all the animals that were alive, Adam could not find a helpmeet. Of course, God knew this, but He waited until Adam real-

---

[59] Helen Schucman, *A Course in Miracles* (Foundation for Inner Peace, 2007), 17-18

ized it. At that point, God put Adam to sleep to take a rib, from which He made "woman" (literally, *man with a womb*). Since God put Adam to sleep for the sole purpose of taking a rib, it is natural to conclude that Adam eventually woke from surgery and saw Eve, much to his delight, I'm sure.

What *Course* is trying to do here are two things:

1. Cast doubt on the normal interpretation of Scripture, *and*
2. Teach that we are all dreaming and need to wake up

If this is reminiscent of the movie trilogy, *The Matrix*, it should be, because this is the essential message of those three movies. While most of the world's population sleeps, only a few have woken from that slumber and are busy creating their own realities.

Books like *A Course in Miracles* are created by intelligent (though fallen) beings from other dimensions. What the average person does not realize is that *Course* is the same lie that Satan used on Eve; however, *Course* is a lie on a grand scale, something that Scientology, for instance, is not.

Course spends a great amount of time redefining what the Bible means by the terms and phrases (doctrines and theology) that we have come to know and understand. It has a new meaning for God, Jesus, the Holy Spirit, the Atonement, and just about everything else that the Bible teaches on a doctrinal or theological subject.

Because of this, it is absolutely clear that the spiritual writer(s) behind *Course* are far more intelligent than, say, the writer(s) behind *The Book of Life*, purported to have been transcribed by Archangel Michael. It is clear from the very foundation and start of *Course* that extremely intelligent beings are being the charade, a charade that works very well for the uninitiated.

Why Should We Believe Them?

Just a quick glance through the book of Daniel or Revelation tells us that not all angels (fallen or non) are equal in might or intelligence.

In the book of Daniel, Gabriel needed the help of (the real) Michael to get past the prince of Persia, who spent 21 days blocking his path so that he could not reach Daniel in answer to Daniel's prayer (cf. Daniel 10).

In the book of Revelation, we know that there are angelic beings of different sizes, shapes, and appearances. This is clear throughout this book. Based on that, it seems reasonable to see that not all of these New Age manifestos or books that support New Age tenets have all been written by beings with the same degree of intelligence.

Regarding the crucifixion, *Course* is not silent. The atonement, through the crucifixion, is actually presented as a personal being. *"I am the only one who can perform miracles indiscriminately, because I am the Atonement."*[60] Along with this, the Atonement was essentially for the purpose of *"cancelling out of all errors that you could not otherwise correct."*[61] We are then told that *"Error cannot really threaten truth, which can always withstand it. Only the error is actually vulnerable. You are free to establish your kingdom where you see fit, but the right choice is inevitable if you remember this:*

> *Spirit is in a state of grace forever.*
> *Your reality is only spirit.*
> *Therefore you are in a state of grace forever."*[62]

The more one reads through *Course*, the more it becomes clear (to those with discernment) that the beings behind the writing of this particular work are absolutely astounding at wordsmithing. They

---

[60] Helen Schucman, *A Course in Miracles* (Foundation for Inner Peace, 2007), 9
[61] Ibid, 9
[62] Ibid, 9-10

take normal speech and orthodox concepts and turn them inside out so that they mean something else entirely.

However, what is fascinating is when they take a statement that is patently false and present it as if it is true. They do this by misdirecting the reader.

For instance, the statement, "*The escape from darkness involves two stages: First, the recognition that **darkness cannot hide**. This step usually entails fear. Second, the recognition that there is nothing you want to hide even if you could. This step brings escape from fear.*"[63]

The phrase "darkness cannot hide" was bolded by me so that you would notice it. It is a statement of nonsense, yet it is placed within other statements that *appear* to be intelligent, therefore the assumption is that this sentence or phrase is also intelligent.

In essence, the point of darkness is not that it can hide, but that it can be *felt*. Darkness in the Bible often connects with evil. Satan's kingdom is referred to as the kingdom of darkness (cf. Colossians 1:13), and as such, whether it is Jesus, Paul, John or someone else referring to it, Satan's kingdom is fully *evil*. This is what makes it dark.

On the other hand, people who die without salvation are said to go to a place of absolute darkness. This darkness causes tremendous fear within people (cf. Matthew 8:12, 22:13, and 25:30). Imagine being in a place where the darkness is so thick you could cut it. Darkness is not meant to hide. It is meant to be felt and experienced.

As far as the atonement is concerned, *Course* teaches that it was not about loss. The atonement is also still going on as well. This statement can be confusing. On one hand, yes, people are still *benefitting* from the atonement, because not only do new people come to know

---

[63] Helen Schucman, *A Course in Miracles* (Foundation for Inner Peace, 2007), 11

Jesus every day through the salvation He made possible because of the atonement, but the atonement will continue to bless the lives of those who believe in Jesus as Savior and Lord throughout this life and into eternity.

Course would have us believe that the actual atonement or crucifixion is ongoing. It is not. *Course* would also have us believe that illness can keep a person temporarily from atonement. The entire teaching of *Course* is related to miracles and healing. It says the atonement heals, and of course it does, but not as *Course* says it does. The atonement is the way in which Jesus lived a perfect life, submitting His life to God the Father every step of the way, and then offered Himself as a propitiation for sin. Those who believe that Jesus is who He said/says He is and that He came to do what He said He did can receive salvation into their life.

This salvation then cancels our sin and causes us to become adopted into God's family. This is the salvation that we speak of, and it was only made possible by the actual, physical crucifixion of Jesus, which we understand to be the atonement. *Course* de-emphasizes the cross of Christ and places the oneness on the person to use the atonement as they would. This is encouraged through the use of miracles that will heal the person so that they can then begin the work of healing the planet and all that this planet contains.

Course defines what is meant by atonement with respect to the crucifixion. *"The crucifixion did not establish the Atonement; the resurrection did. Many sincere Christians have misunderstood this. No one who is free of the belief in scarcity could possibly make this mistake. If the crucifixion is seen from an upside-down point of view, it does appear as if God permitted and even encouraged one of His Sons to suffer because he was good."*

It also must be clearly noted that *Course* teaches that God has only one Son. It goes on to teach that *all* are part of the Son. In other words, all people are part of the divine. Since this is the case, then to subject anyone to the crucifixion as a means of suffering is against the view of God that *Course* teaches.

Here again, we are being misdirected. In truth, all of Jesus' life – His actual day-to-day living, His trial, His beating, His death, *and* His resurrection – work together.

Had not Jesus lived a perfect life, He could not have offered Himself as atonement for our sin. Had He not died a sinner's death, He would not have fulfilled Isaiah 52-53 where it speaks of the Suffering Servant. Had He not fulfilled that part of the plan of redemption, He would not have been found worthy to rise from the dead.

The entire reason Jesus died was to allow God the Father's wrath to be poured out on Him *instead of on us*. People say that they have a problem with the "substitutionary atonement." I would too, *IF* the person who died had not been God Himself. If God had simply picked a human being to be the propitiation for our sin, it would have seemed strange, to say the least.

However, in the eternal council of the Godhead, prior to the foundations of the world, God determined that He would become a human being Himself, live a perfect life in complete fulfillment of the entire law, and then, after having done so, would offer Himself as the Substitute so that we would not have to die in our sin and be eternally separated from God.

This is the miracle of the atonement, which simply culminates in the resurrection. The crucifixion was so important to the entire process of redemption because through it, God effectively dealt with sin by pouring out His wrath on a perfect Lamb without blemish, and a volunteer Lamb at that.

Course wants us to believe that the crucifixion has little to do with it and dwelling on it can create undue fear within people over who God is and how He relates to humanity. On the contrary, when we rightly understand the true purpose of the crucifixion *and* we understand that it was God Himself who did the suffering on our behalf, this truth chases away all fear and causes us to begin to comprehend the love of God.

The being who speaks throughout *Course* claims not only to be the atonement, but also claims to be the *"lamb of God who taketh away the sins of the world."*[64] Therefore, this being is masquerading as God the Son.

Throughout *Course*, everything is related to *perception*. For instance, we are told that after the final judgment there will be no more. Why? We are told it is *"because beyond perception there is no judgment."*[65] This statement is gobbledy-gook. It makes no sense. In truth, beyond perception is *nothing*. One who does not perceive does not exist.

Course tries to break this down further by providing an example. *"When you feel tired, it is because you have judged yourself as capable of being tired."* No, it is because our bodies are physical and therefore need rest and sleep to recuperate from being awake all day.

When Jesus and the apostles were in the Garden of Gethsemane, the apostles fell asleep. Jesus' response to this was to say that the spirit was willing, but the flesh was weak (cf. Matthew 26:40-43). He was not saying this because the apostles had somehow never managed to understand that if they simply judged themselves to be awake, they would have been. Jesus said this because it is the truth of the matter.

---

[64] Helen Schucman, *A Course in Miracles* (Foundation for Inner Peace, 2007), 37
[65] Ibid, 46

Why Should We Believe Them?

Our spirits – or our willingness – are often much more agreeable to doing something than our flesh is because our bodies grow tired and they experience hunger, thirst, and even pain. This does not mean that we have somehow failed to comprehend the deep spiritual truths of the universe. It is simply the way our bodies tell us what they need.

Science tells us we can live approximately five days without water before we die. I challenge anyone who thoroughly believes what *Course* teaches and who has been a practitioner of it for some time to try to go without water for ten days, or fifteen days. Don't drink anything, and when your body starts screaming at you because it is literally dying of thirst, just tell yourself that you are thirsty because you have judged yourself thirsty. Knowing that, judge yourself *not* thirsty.

Oh yes, there are times in the Bible when both Moses and Jesus did not have food at least for many, many days. In Jesus' temptation (cf. Matthew 4), He got very hungry. Instead of trying to tell Himself that He really wasn't hungry, the Tempter came along and tried to get Him to use His deity to create food for Himself. Jesus did not give into the temptation, but He was *still* hungry.

It was only after Satan left Him did the angels come and minister to Him, and at that point, in Matthew 4, it is likely that they restored His strength with food.

Just because we think we can create or transform our reality from what it is into something else does not mean that we can actually do that. I can build things. I can create things in Photoshop. I can write another book using Word. There are many things I can do, but I cannot use my will or any alleged energy I have to create something that is not.

Why Should We Believe Them?

The Matrix was a good science fiction movie. However, when people start looking at it as if that is kind of what our life is like, problems begin. Decades ago, people went to see movies for the sheer entertainment of them. While some certainly got carried away with the lives of celebrities (as many do today), there was a separation between what was real and what was not real.

If you went to see a horror movie, you might become very scared at times throughout the movie, but you did not leave thinking that Frankenstein or Dracula was going to attack you as you walked home. People knew the difference between what they saw on the screen and what they experienced in real life.

Of course, some will mention the Orson Wells' "War of the Worlds" scenario. But what made that particular situation so real to many is that they tuned in *after* the program started and missed the part about it being a fictional account of an attack from outer space.

People heard what they thought were real news broadcasts and they were horrified. It was the reality of the situation, as far as their hearing went, that prompted them to think the situation itself was real. Because they thought they were listening to actual news reports and not a radio show, they became fearful.

But going to see a horror movie, people know that what they are watching is faked. It is a form of entertainment and that's that. In today's society, though, while horror movies are still entertainment for some, they have essentially crossed over into areas that are somewhat real.

For instance, the movie *Splice* is about a team of scientists who do experiments that wind up crossing human DNA with other life forms. We know that scientists in real life have been playing with DNA for some time and have in fact cloned sheep and other things. Could they be working behind the scene to do other things with DNA? It's certainly possible, so a film like *Splice,* while a thriller of sorts, is based on something that reflects what is happening in real life.

No one goes to a horror movie anymore and is taken in by bad effects and unbelievable plots. Frankenstein won't work today and neither would Dracula. The movie series *Underworld* is something that people find hard to believe. *Blade* is the same way. These movies about human vampires have an unbelievable storyline. The reason they are somewhat successful at the box office has to do with the quality of effects and the story itself.

Today's horror fan needs something they can really be enamored with and something that will cause them to believe it is possible. This is why more and more horror movies are including the sci-fi aspect of things, because that by itself makes the movie more believable.

Something like *The Matrix* is something everyone can relate to, up to a point. We've all had jobs we didn't like. We all have mundane parts to our life. We want something fresh, exciting, and new.

The Matrix comes along and tells us in a very believable way that life is simply one huge dream, and if we will only wake up from that dream, we will be able to strike out on our own to create the reality that we wish to create. That is the message of *The Matrix.* While people know that the world of *The Matrix* does not exist, there is still this sense that humanity needs to be wakened to what is real.

Course follows this line of thinking, and since it came before *The Matrix*, people who have seen the movies and read *Course* will put two and two together and see what they can do to make their life more to their liking.

I am amazed at how many times *Course* refers to biblical concepts, yet changes their meaning. In doing so, the concepts become changed altogether into absurdity, but that does not stop *Course* from moving onward. In fact, actual truth means little to *Course* because so much time is spent trying to change the truth of the Bible into something else entirely that its bold attempts to do this simply come across as strength. In other words, because the new meaning is often so outlandish, people are tempted to think that it must be true simply because it is so unique.

In referring to the branch that doesn't bear fruit being cut off, *Course* states, "*Be glad! The light will shine from the true Foundation of life, and your own thought system will stand corrected.*"[66] In John 15, Jesus starts off by saying that He is the true vine. Here He likens Himself as a plant for the purposes of painting a mental picture.

Immediately following this statement, He says, "*Every branch in me that beareth not fruit he taketh away: and every branch that beareth fruit, he purgeth it, that it may bring forth more fruit*" (v. 2). This is not a good thing, as *Course* would have us believe. Jesus is the vine and people represent individual branches. Those branches that do not bear fruit are hacked off, taken away, and **burned in the fire** (cf. Matthew 7:19; emphasis added).

Gee, *Course* doesn't tell you this part, does it? It says that the branches that make all of you as one being are cut off, and that will benefit you in the end.

That's not what the Bible says. It tells us a different story, that Jesus is the vine and each individual branch represents individual people. Those people who do not bear fruit will be cut off, leaving only those who *do* bear fruit to remain. The ones that are cut off are burned up, and this represents the second, eternal death after judgment.

---

[66] Helen Schucman, *A Course in Miracles* (Foundation for Inner Peace, 2007), 51

Repeatedly throughout *Course* we see where the Bible is mishandled and misappropriated. *"The Bible says that you should go with a brother twice as far as he asks."*[67] No, that is not what the Bible says at all. It sounds familiar though, doesn't it? It makes people think that since there is so much that is familiar here in *Course* that reminds us of the biblical text, then it must be right on in its interpretation. Unfortunately, it is wrong. It is no different than the preacher who recently declared that the world was to end on May 21st. When that day came and went without judgment occurring, a new date of October 21st was given.

This particular preacher said he arrived at his conclusion through careful Bible study and figuring the dates mathematically. Unfortunately, as I read through his arguments, it was clear that he was not on solid ground from the beginning. Yes, he used the Bible, but no, he did not understand it or interpret it correctly. He either read into the text or misappropriated meanings of the text to use in his scenario.

This is exactly what *Course* does, and it is extremely blatant about it as well. The interesting thing of course is that the information and teaching is produced in such a matter-of-fact way that the average person will not see through it, especially if they do not know their Bible.

Where did the writer of *Course* get the idea that the Bible teaches we should go twice as far with a brother as he asks? From the Sermon on the Mount. Matthew 5:41 says, *"And whosoever shall compel thee to go a mile, go with him twain."* Notice the text uses the word "compel," which is generally understood to mean "to force." During the days of Jesus' time, Roman soldiers were allowed to grab a person and force them to carry their pack, but the law said they only had to

---

[67] Helen Schucman, *A Course in Miracles* (Foundation for Inner Peace, 2007), 52

carry it one mile. Jesus' point was that though they are in control for the first mile, carry it another mile without being asked or forced, because this turns the tables. It also opens the door for witnessing to that soldier.

A Roman soldier was not considered a "brother" to a Jewish person. They hated the Romans and the feeling was mutual. If a Jewish person was forced to carry a pack, you can bet that at the exact end of that mile, they would drop that pack like it was on fire and move on. Jesus went beyond that, telling them they should carry it on their own, using it as a way to regain respect from the soldier *and* as an opportunity for evangelism.

Course would have us believe that this incident and instruction from Jesus really dealt with two brothers. Sorry, but that's not the case. Once you begin to get beyond all the flowery language of *Course* and strip it down to its meat and potatoes, you begin to see how much this book is trying to pull the wool over the eyes of the average person.

One last section related to *Course* is the way it explains what salvation is all about, and included in that is the crucifixion. From the Bible, we know that just as Jesus explained, salvation starts with being born from above, or being born again (cf. John 3). We know this because of the conversation Jesus had with Nicodemus, a Pharisee who came to see Jesus at night because he was more than curious about Jesus and what He taught.

We also know from Paul that to become saved (or born again) a person needs to believe on Jesus. *"That if thou shalt confess with thy mouth the Lord Jesus, and shalt believe in thine heart that God hath raised him from the dead, thou shalt be saved. For with the heart man believeth unto righteousness; and with the mouth confession is made unto salvation"* (Romans 10:9-10)

Course teaches that the actual crucifixion was not punishment at all. *"The crucifixion is nothing more than an extreme example. Its value, like the value of any teaching device, lies solely in the kind of learning it facilitates. It can be, and has been, misunderstood. This is only because the fearful are apt to perceive fearfully. I have already told you that you can also call on me to share my decision, and thus make it stronger. I have also told you that the crucifixion was the last useless journey the Sonship need take, and that it represents release from fear to anyone who understands it. While I emphasized only the resurrection before, the purpose of the crucifixion and how it actually led to the resurrection was not clarified then. Nevertheless, it has a definite contribution to make to your own life, and if you will consider it without fear, it will help you understand your own role as a teacher.*

"...The real meaning of the crucifixion lies in the apparent *intensity of the assault of some of the Sons of God upon another. This, of course, is impossible, and must be fully understood as impossible. Otherwise, I cannot serve as a model for learning.*

"...The message the crucifixion was intended to teach was that it is not necessary to perceive any form of assault in persecution, because you cannot *be persecuted. If you respond in anger, you must be equating yourself with the destructible, and are therefore regarding yourself insanely.*

"...You are not asked to be crucified, which was part of my example in the face of so much less extreme temptations to misperceive, and not to accept them as false justifications for anger. There can be no justification for the unjustifiable. Do not believe there is, and do not teach that there is. Remember always that what you believe you will teach. Believe with me, and we will become equal as teachers."[68]

---

[68] Helen Schucman, *A Course in Miracles* (Foundation for Inner Peace, 2007), 93

Why Should We Believe Them?

This whole line of reasoning, if you can call it that, reminds of some of the statements made in the movie *Mystery Men*. It was a movie based on normal individuals who believed they were superheroes. These men and women worked together to take on the criminals such as Casanova Frankenstein in their world. The main good guy – Captain Amazing – is taken out by Casanova, leaving the other good guys. Problem is that they need some help, so they get a guy called The Sphinx to train and lead them.

Throughout his time teaching the regular guys to become more like superheroes, he would say things like, "*until you learn to master your rage, your rage will become your master*" and "*when you learn to balance a tack hammer on your head, you will head off your foes with a balanced attack.*"

There are many legitimate examples of this type of saying, such as when Jesus said, "*The Sabbath was made for man, and not man for the Sabbath*," (cf. Mark 2:27) or John F. Kennedy's statement, "*Ask not what your country can do for you; ask what you can do for your country.*" However, it is clear that there are many asinine examples of them as well, and the two quoted from the movie *Mystery Men* point that out.

Course uses a form of this nonsensical speaking that can *sound* mysterious and therefore intelligent. When it comes down to it, though, there is not a great deal of meaning in the verbiage that's presented.

Take the middle paragraph of the most recent quote from *Course*: "*The message the crucifixion was intended to teach was that it is not necessary to perceive any form of assault in persecution, because you* cannot *be persecuted. If you respond in anger, you must be equating yourself with the destructible, and are therefore regarding yourself insanely.*" I'm sure there will be people who read this and respond to it with a "whoa, heavy," but in truth, *what* is being stated there?

Why Should We Believe Them?

First, we are told that we cannot be persecuted. If we see ourselves as being persecuted, the natural response to that is one of anger. If that is our response, we are then seeing ourselves as something that can be destroyed and therefore we have gone crazy. If it were true that life is merely perception and the reality that is associated with this life is the perception of either our making or someone else's, then this statement may have at least a modicum of merit.

In essence, then, Jesus died because He was providing an example of what persecution *looks* like to those who miss the point that persecution does not actually exist.

But this is all predicated on the idea that life is an illusion and nothing is real. Since this is the case, we can create what we want to be real and it *will* be real.

If we are being persecuted, it is because we have created a situation in which we are persecuting ourselves. It is not real. Since it is not real, why waste the time to create something that cannot possibly exist anyway?

Course desperately tries to define an alternate reality, one that is based on nonsense, but it tries to do that in a very intelligent-sounding way so that people will perceive the teachings of *Course* as worthy of consideration and therefore worthy of doing.

A Course in Miracles is a book that is so deep into the New Age that it could well be a truncated form of everything that both Blavatsky and Bailey wrote. No, I'm not claiming *Course* violates copyright laws by plagiarizing from these other works. I'm simply saying that what took Blavatsky and Bailey volumes to describe is described in *Course* in far fewer volumes.

In the end, *Course* teaches people the same lie that Satan used in the Garden of Eden when he confronted Eve and Adam. It really is nothing more than "you are gods, so live like you are." That's it in a nutshell, and this is the battle cry of the New Age movement. It deigns to tell people that they are god and are quite capable of creating their own reality if they will simply do away with the age old antiquated beliefs of orthodox Christianity.

This is why aliens, ascended masters, and all the rest *must* attack Christianity. They cannot leave Christianity intact, because if they do, people will become *saved* as they recognize their need for the Savior.

People who recognize that they need Jesus and the only salvation that is available understand that what the Bible teaches is *true*. Those who can be persuaded that the Bible is not true, that Jesus is not God (in the sense that He is normally understood to be God), that there is really no such thing as sin, and that life itself is merely a perception that can be changed, will find delightful words and concepts in a book like *A Course in Miracles*.

Ultimately, like every area of New Age theology and Alienology, the concept that all people are connected in one giant sum of all our parts is the main tenet that teaches people that their worth or value is found in the *sum*. Because of this, there is no real sense of individual value apart from other people.

It is the Christian who removes him/herself from the picture, going off on a different path, who is really the problem. It is the authentic Christian that is also actually in danger of never learning or understanding the teachings of the universe, according to *Course*. The universe tells us we are one of many and together we make up the universal whole.

Jesus tells us He knows the number of hairs on our head and that we are uniquely loved by Him, so much so, in fact, that He willingly died so that we could receive eternal life from Him.

The gobbledy-gook that passes for New Age intelligence is nothing more than infantile pabulum. It breeds nothing except a heart of disillusionment, passing itself off as wisdom of the ages. It's nothing of the sort, and I pray that God will open the eyes of people who believe it to be something brilliant and beyond measure.

It is a lie, and the lie is perpetrated by demons posing as ascended masters and aliens. After all, who would believe a demon if it showed itself or presented itself as a demon?

SO WHAT'S THE TRUTH?

Every person has a great deal to gain or a great deal to lose depending upon which "truth" they choose to follow. Of course, there is only *one* truth, and this is exactly why Jesus says to make every effort to enter into the narrow gate (cf. Matthew 7:13; Luke 13:24), because it is that gate and that gate alone that leads to eternal life. There is no other gate that leads to life eternal.

Why Should We Believe Them?

Like me, you have a choice before you. You can believe all of the noise that emanates from the spiritual plane from inter-dimensional beings, or you can believe what the Bible teaches. It is your decision completely and one would think that a decision of this magnitude would require all the evidence one could find.

Is that what you have done? Have you taken the time to research the reasons why you believe what you believe (even if it's nothing), or have you based your beliefs ultimately on how you *feel* about something?

To you, the idea of aliens may sound plausible. The idea of a God who allows people to spend eternity in hell may not sound as plausible. So you are basing a literal life or death decision on apparently *plausibility?*

In this last chapter, I would like to spend some time to compare statements, claims, and propositions from each side, and then I want to take the time to look at anything that provides evidence or even proof for each position. Are you willing to do that? Are you willing to take your beliefs and place them under the microscope? You should be and I hope you are, because in truth, your eternity does rest on whether or not you have made the correct choice.

There is a lot of information that is thrown at you every day. A good deal of that information is incorrect and it is important that you learn and know how to tell the difference.

There are some facts about God – and yes, these facts are based on the Bible – that you need to know. They are:

1. **God is love**. Because of this, it is truthful to say that God loves *you*.
2. **God is forgiving**. Since God is forgiving, He has obviously determined a way that you and I can come back to Him in faith

and have all of our sin – past, present, and future – forever forgiven.
3. **God is just**. Because God is just, He cannot simply ignore sinful acts and sin itself. If He did that, He would be no more just than a corrupt judge who, though a criminal was found fully guilty of his crimes, lets him walk.
4. **God is holy**. God's holiness allows Him to act on our behalf.

One of the most important questions you should be asking yourself is this one: *why do these works from ascended masters always seem to simply focus on the character of the Bible, or Jesus?*

In other words, if you take just about any book or article that's been written by alleged ascended masters, they often denigrate Scripture, either directly or indirectly. As far as I know, they have never taken exception to the Qur'an or other works that people consider to be holy.

It is always the Bible. Somehow, they say, we have missed the meaning, so they need to straighten us out on that score. It's the same with Jesus. Somehow, we got it wrong. Jesus was only "a god" insofar as we can also be gods. He wasn't or isn't *the* God. In fact, that God does not exist, according to aliens/ascended masters. It's a hoax perpetrated by people who have simply failed to understand the Bible.

Christianity, the orthodox view of Scripture, Jesus as God, the Holy Spirit as God, God the Father as God – all of these things need clarification, we are told, and that seems to be their first order of business as they reveal themselves to humanity, making the rounds from person to person or group to group.

Isn't that strange? Doesn't that strike you as odd? I'm sure it doesn't if you're an atheist or agnostic. It may make perfect sense to you, but in truth, it doesn't. For centuries, authentic Christians have been telling the world that there is only one way to God and the only salvation that is offered, and that is through the atonement provided by Jesus. He said it Himself in John 14 and we are merely repeating what He said originally.

That's not right, though, according to beings from beyond. That's not what Jesus meant. In effect, these beings are here to tell us that it is the exact opposite. Just as Christians have been telling the world that there is only one way to God (through Jesus) and everything else is wrong, inter-dimensional beings are here to tell us that everything is correct and *Christianity* is wrong.

In essence, that should not even matter to them, but it seems to the highest priority on their "to do" list. Instead of helping the world become a better place *physically*, they insist that first things are first and they must help the world become a better place *spiritually*.

This means that because they are not providing any real answers to the very real problems the world faces, millions die each year. That does not seem to matter to them at all. Oh well, it's just a way that the earth is cleansing itself. These individuals who die come back as something else or they go to another place where they can start anew. No worries.

If that's the truth, then authentic Christians have not only been wasting their time, but too many have died for the cause of Jesus and did not need to do that. The fact remains that these ascended masters or aliens have spent their time wowing us with their highly advanced technology, but instead of enlightening us about that, feel the need to warn us that we had better get spiritually on track. If we fail, we will destroy ourselves.

The idiocy of these types of statements that allegedly come from other dimensions or worlds is beyond the pale, yet these and many other statements are routinely accepted as truth. But the problem continues that within the spiritual realm – connected with our spiritual growth – things can take a long time.

People cannot change patterns of thought or behavior overnight. Yet if we had the right technology that could feed the world, or allow us to conserve and use our resources far better than we do, wouldn't that be worth sharing? After this, *then* they could take the time to show us where we have allegedly gone wrong spiritually.

This is not the way they are doing things, though. They say they care about us and do not want us to destroy ourselves. Yet, it is fine that millions die every year through all types of sicknesses, natural disasters, and famines. Does that make sense to you? It certainly does not make sense to me.

I want to be as spiritually mature as the next person, which is why I take my relationship with Jesus seriously. I believe that when I became a Christian, the Holy Spirit – God – took up residence within me and began guiding me from that point onward so that my character would begin mirroring the character of Jesus.

People who are involved in aspects of the New Age movement also want to better themselves spiritually. The difference is that they must work at it, whereas what I must do is submit my will to Him, giving Him room to work in my life.

We both want to improve spiritually. We both want to love people more. We both want to see the problems of this world evaporate. New Agers believe they must work to accomplish that, whereas the authentic Christian believes he/she must submit to the Lord so that the Lord will work in and through him/her to accomplish His purposes.

The New Age is involved in what they believe to be impersonal forces. They believe these forces can work to change them. I agree that this is what will happen, but I do not agree that these forces are impersonal. Certainly, the beings they encounter are very personal, yet we are to believe that it is not those beings who attempt to correct their behavior and attitude. It is an impersonal force that apparently does that.

The New Age adherent really answers to no one except themselves, and when they begin to do that, they begin to see themselves as their own god. This is in effect what they are becoming. They answer to no one and they do not need to submit themselves to anyone. They simply follow a prescribed path laid out for them by these intelligent beings.

In other words, the New Age boils down to a pattern of thinking, but what people fail to see is that this pattern of thinking is really no different than the pattern that Satan (through the Tempter) wanted Eve and Adam to think. "See yourselves as gods!" he said. "Cast off the heavy load that God has placed on your shoulders! Be free to create what YOU want to create!"

In the Garden of Eden, Satan knew he could not go to either Adam or Eve and tell them God did not exist and instead it was some impersonal force that guided life and the universe. Satan knew that he could not use the lie that told them that aliens created life and that God was really nothing more than an alien collective that determined to create something new as a huge experiment. He knew none of these things would work.

The only way Satan could successfully cause Eve and then Adam to sin was by using the lie that says that God was not what He professed to be. By calling God a liar, that doubt could create the perfect situation that would allow both Eve and Adam to believe the Tempter and disbelieve God.

Satan had very little room to work at all, because both Adam and Eve saw God, they walked with God, and they heard Him speak to them on a daily basis. They saw the Creation in all its glory. They tasted food as none of us have tasted or will taste it until we get to heaven with Him. Both Adam and Eve knew what God was like. For someone to come along and say that God did not exist was foolhardy. That person would be laughed out of the garden.

So Satan did the only thing that was left for him to do: create doubt. He did this and won – a huge but temporary victory.

Today, there are so many other ways that Satan has at his disposal that he can use to cause people to sin. He can help them believe God does not exist at all. He can help them understand that God must not really be a loving God at all because of all the evil in the world.

Satan can call God one lie after another and he will craft that lie to cater to the unique personality of each person. He doesn't mind doing that if it keeps another one from salvation.

The greatest lie that Satan has at his disposal now – aside from the one that says God does not exist – is the lie that says that God is not personal, but in reality is an impersonal force. All we need to do is tap into that force and we will become gods ourselves.

Years ago, with the movie "Star Wars," the world became familiar with "the force." This force was impersonal and there for our benefit. It also had two sides, the good side and the evil side. Each person makes up their own mind about which side they want to be on, and even in "Star Wars," it seemed that many people were not even really aware of this force.

Since these movies have come out, creator George Lucas has built an empire based on them. Many have said that the movies reflect his personal beliefs. Whether that is true or not, the reality seems to be that there are plenty of creative people in either business or in Hollywood who likely believe that they have crafted their own realities.

In so doing, they have come to believe that they have the power to do what books like *Course* tell them they *can* do.

Whenever any book, article, movie, or song tells us that we can create our own reality, it is part of the New Age mystique. People love to hear it because it frees us from the idea that God – a personal God – is in control of all things.

People rebel against the idea that there is one superior Being called God who knows everything and can be everywhere at once and who also controls what happens in the universe. People do not like that because just as Lucifer (who became Satan) chafed at having to exist under God's command, people do the same thing.

It seems that beings with a free will ultimately use that will to turn away from God. As far as I am aware, the only beings who have not are what the Bible refers to as the elect angels of God (cf. 1 Tim). These beings appear to never have had a problem with not wanting to stay loyal to God. It is clear that they are elect because they were created that way, and because of that they do not even think about the possibility of not doing what God wants.

However, God made creatures with free will, and every one of those creatures has at one time or another turned away from God. The angels that became fallen had free will. Adam and Eve fell because they followed their free will away from God. Satan himself, who had been created perfect, but with free will, opted to one day think that he was far better than the God of all Creation.

Free will sets itself up against God in rebellion. If the history of the nation of Israel is not a perfect case in point, then nothing will be. Throughout Israel's history, God had to repeatedly purge the rebels from the camp because in spite of how often they saw God work to provide food, water, or to protect them, they wanted to overthrow

Moses. When this happened, God stepped in and took care of the rebellion.

Had these individuals not had free will, the thought of overthrowing Moses would never have entered their minds. They would have simply gone along with what Moses told them, knowing it was the right thing to do, and would not have experienced the desire to push their own ideas and wants.

Free will makes people susceptible to sin. Sin is lawlessness and it is rebellion. It is possible to have free will and not sin. Jesus showed that it was possible because not once did He sin. For the average person, it is not possible, even for those who become authentic Christians. As one myself, I still make mistakes. I still sin from time to time. I will, unfortunately, sin from time to time in the future. Why is this? It is because I have a sin nature, and by its very nature it is opposed to God. My sin nature works together with my "free will" (such as it is) and decides to choose against God's plans.

As far as human beings are concerned, only Adam, Eve, and Jesus had perfect free wills. When they were created (or in the case of Jesus, when He was born into this world as a human being), their free wills had not yet chosen against God.

Temptation is the very thing that Satan uses to engage our free will to choose against God. He succeeded with both Adam and Eve, but He failed miserably and continually where Jesus is concerned. Jesus never once used His free will to go against God the Father.

Because Adam and Eve fell through the use of their free will, that free will became corrupted. They deliberately chose to go against the prescribed revealed will of God. The free will that we have is not the same free will that they had. It is far more susceptible to falling because of its corrupt nature. It is that much more difficult for us to ignore the demands of our free will because it is often energized by our sin nature.

There is only one way back to God, and it is the way that Jesus opened for you. He did that through His sacrificial death on the cross and it was not meant as an example. It was meant to deal a death blow to sin and judgment, but only those who take advantage of it will enjoy eternal life. It is really that simple, yet so often missed.

There is no reason to fear God if you understand that because of God the Son, Jesus, true forgiveness has been made available to you. Your sins can be canceled forever.

Do you know when you will die? Are you aware of the day and hour when you will slip from this life into eternity? I bet you do not know when that will happen. So why are you living as if you **_do_** *know when it will happen?* Putting a decision about Jesus off until another day is taking a huge chance because of the fact that you do not know when you will die. That is plainly simple, and logic alone demands that you do not put this decision off. Yet you do, because the thought of becoming a Christian makes you feel uncomfortable.

You wrongly believe that to become a Christian means that you have to change in a major way *before* Jesus will accept you. It means to you giving up the things you love now because if you love them, then obviously they are wrong and God does not love them.

You are putting the cart before the horse. You must understand that God is not rejecting you. He is not standing there, tapping His foot, demanding that you eliminate those things that He does not like before you can come to Him for salvation.

If you (or anyone) could do that, you would not *need* His salvation at all. It is because you and I do things that are not pleasing to Him that we need His salvation.

What do you do that you would like to no longer do? Do you drink excessively until you cannot control it? Do you play around with drugs? Do you eat too much food until you have become overweight, lethargic and sickly?

What other things are in your life that you do not like? Are you drawn to illicit extra-marital affairs? Do you have a problem with lust? Are you a shopaholic? Do you tend to tell lies a great deal because it makes you feel important, or to hide things about your life?

Do you find that you do not like people and you would prefer to be around animals or out in the woods than around people? Are you a workaholic? Do you place a high value on money and you find that you work very hard to obtain it?

Here's the problem. The enemy of our souls comes to us and tells us that God will never accept us until we get rid of those things. He lies to us that God essentially wants us "perfect" before He will be willing to meet us and grant us eternal life. This is completely untrue.

The other lie that our enemy tells us is that we should not become a Christian because the fun in our life will fly out the door. We will no longer be able to drink or do the fun things we enjoy now. We start to think that coming to God means becoming a doormat for people and having to fill our life with things we do not want to *ever* do.

These are all lies, and unfortunately, too many people believe them. First of all, God does not expect you to be "perfect" before you come to Him for salvation. If that were the case, no one would be able to ever approach Him.

Secondly, God does not say that He is going to take away all the things we enjoy and replace them with things we hate. What is wrong with enjoying the lake on your boat? What is wrong with spending a day with the family fishing or just relaxing in the mountains? There is nothing wrong with these things.

What God *will* do is begin to remove the things that have ensnared you so that life is actually draining from you, but you are not aware of it. For instance, maybe you drink excessively and you have tried everything you can think of to quit. You have gone to AA meetings, spent thousands of dollars on this program or that, and you have even used your own will power to free yourself from the addiction to alcohol, all to no avail.

The question is not: *do I need to quit before I come to Jesus?* The question is: *am I willing to allow Him to work in and through me to take away the addiction I have to alcohol?* Do you see the difference? Are you willing to allow Him to work in you to break that addiction so that you will become a healthier person, one who is able to think straight and one who learns to rely on Him for strength? That is all He wants you to be able to do. He knows you cannot break that addiction (or any addiction for that matter) with your own strength and willpower. Are you willing to allow Him to do it in and through you?

What if you are a workaholic? What if you have "things" like a boat, a house in Cancun, a large bank account, four cars, and more? Do you think that God is going to ask you to give it up, or worse, do you think that God will simply come in and take all of that from you? I know of nothing in Scripture that tells us He will do that.

What God will do with all of those who come to Him trusting Him for salvation is one thing, which begins the moment we receive salvation and will continue until the day we stand before Him. He will begin to create within us the character of Jesus (cf. Ephesians 2:10).

Here is a verse from the Old Testament that was said originally through the prophet Ezekiel to the people of Israel. While this was specifically stated to the Jews, it is applicable to all who receive salvation through Jesus Christ.

"I will give you a new heart and put a new spirit within you; I will take the heart of stone out of your flesh and give you a heart of flesh. I will put My Spirit within you and cause you to walk in My statutes, and you will keep My judgments and do them" (Ezekiel 36:26-27).

God is speaking here through Ezekiel, and He is saying that He will give the people a new heart of flesh, removing that old heart of stone. This is God's responsibility. God is the One who makes that happen. We are told in the book of Hebrews that God is the Author and Finisher of our faith (cf. Hebrews 12:2). This tells me that God is the One who changes me from within so that over time, my desires are slowly turned into His desires.

I recall years ago thinking that God wanted to do everything in my life that I did not want Him to do. I fell into the asinine belief that He wanted to change everything about me. What I learned is that yes, there are things that God does want to change about me. However, there is a lot that God originally gave me that He has also enhanced and used for His glory.

Maybe you are a workaholic who thinks that working hard is something God does not want you to do. This is not necessarily the case. He may have given you the ability and the knowledge to work in the area of finance for a great purpose. All He may wind up doing is dialing back your workaholic tendencies so that you have more time to enjoy your family and study His Word.

But you say you smoke, or drink, or use illegal drugs, and you don't want to give those up. As I stated, you can't give those up under your own power, and the fact that you have tried so many times has proven it to you.

But God knows what is and what is not good for you. Are you willing to *allow* Him to work in you to change your desires so that you no longer want to smoke, use illegal drugs, or drink nearly as much?

Why Should We Believe Them?

Then you say that you believe God wants to make you a Christian so you can become miserable. Isn't that what most Christians are; miserable? Not the Christians I know, and certainly not me, my wife, or our children.

Where does the Bible say that God wants us miserable? You will not find it. What God wants is for us to be blessed, and that begins when we receive salvation from His hand.

You know, if we would stop and take the time to consider the fact that this life is exceedingly short if we compare it to eternity, we will then realize that there is nothing so important that it should keep us from receiving Jesus as Savior and Lord.

Unfortunately, too many people do not consider the brevity of life. They think they will live forever, or at the very least, they will die when they are really old and gray. That will come too soon. This author is going to be 54 years old in just a few months from this writing. It truly seems like yesterday that I was a young boy fishing in the Delaware River near Hobart, New York. There I spent many Saturdays fishing and simply enjoying being outdoors. How did life go by so very quickly? How could that have happened?

It has happened, and I am at a point in life where not only do I realize that this life is short, but I actually look forward to spending eternity with Jesus after this life. Does that sound morbid to you? It shouldn't, because by comparing this life to eternity, we should get a sense of what is truly important.

God does not expect us to become Mother Theresas. He does not necessarily expect us to give up everything and become missionaries in outer Mongolia. What God expects is for us to simply allow Him to change our character as He sees fit.

Over time, we may well find that we have simply stopped swearing without realizing it. Our desire for cigarettes or alcohol has nearly evaporated. Illicit affairs no longer enter the picture.

We also may find that some of the things we want to eliminate in our life become more pronounced. Often the enemy will do this to cause us to focus on something that God is not even doing in our lives at that point. It causes tension, frustration, and self-anger.

If you have gotten to this point in your life and you have not dealt with the question about Jesus, it is about time you do so. You need to stop what you are doing and realize a couple of things before you go through another minute in this life.

- **Sinner**: you need to realize that you are a sinner. You have sinned and you will continue to sin. Sin is breaking the laws that God has set up. We all sin. We have all broken God's laws and that breaks any connection we might have had with God. Sin pushes us away from Him.

    Romans 3:23 says *"For all have sinned, and come short of the glory of God."* That means you and that means me. All means all. That is the first step. We need to recognize and agree with God that yes, we are sinners. I'm a sinner. You are a sinner. This results in God's anger, what the Bible terms "wrath."

- **God's Wrath**: Romans 1:18 says, *"For the wrath of God is revealed from heaven against all ungodliness and unrighteousness of men, who suppress the truth in unrighteousness."*

    This is as much a fact as the truth that we are all sinners. Because we are sinners – by breaking God's law(s) – God has every right to be angry with us and ultimately destroy that which is sinful. If we choose to remain "in" our sinful states throughout this life, we will – unfortunately – be destroyed with the rest of sin.

Fortunately, there *is* a remedy, and it is salvation.

- **God's Gift**: In the sixteenth chapter of Acts, a jailer asks Paul this famous question: *what must I do to be saved?* The question was asked because Paul and Barnabas had been imprisoned, and while there, they began singing praises to God.

God then sent a powerful earthquake that opened the doors to all the prison cells, yet no one escaped. When the jailer arrived, he saw that everyone was still in their cells, and after seeing that miracle (what prisoner would not want to escape from prison?), turned and asked what he must do to be saved. He was speaking of the spiritual aspect of things. He wanted to know how he could be guaranteed eternal life.

The answer Paul gave the man was, "*Believe on the Lord Jesus Christ, and thou shalt be saved, and thy house*" (Acts 16:31).

This is not head knowledge or intellectual assent. This is *believing from the heart.* In fact, Paul makes a very similar statement in another book he wrote, Romans. He says, "*That if thou shalt confess with thy mouth the Lord Jesus, and shalt believe in thine heart that God hath raised him from the dead, thou shalt be saved. For with the heart man believeth unto righteousness; and with the mouth confession is made unto salvation*" (Romans 10:9-10).

When we fully believe something, we confess that it is true. It must begin in the heart because that is where the will is located. We must want to believe. We must endeavor to believe.

We must seek to believe.

We must stop giving ourselves all the reasons to deny or ignore Jesus. As God, He became a Man, born of a virgin. He clothed Himself with humanity that He might show us how to live, and in so doing, would keep every portion of the law.

If Jesus was capable of keeping every portion of the law, then He would be found worthy to become a sacrifice for our sin – yours and mine. If He became a sacrifice for our sin, then all that we must do is embrace Him and His sacrificial death.

In short then, to become saved we must:

1. *Admit (we sin)*
2. *Repent (want to turn away from it)*
3. *Believe (that Jesus is the answer)*
4. *Embrace (the truth about Jesus)*

We **admit** that we are sinner, that we have sinned. This is nothing more than agreeing with God that we have broken His law. Can you honestly say that you have not broken God's law? If you admit to breaking even the "smallest" law, then you are a lawbreaker.

After we admit that we have sinned, the next step is found in **repenting**. Some believe that repenting is actually moving away from sin. This author believes that it is a willingness to move away from sin, and there is a difference.

As we have already discussed, it is impossible to stop sinning. Human beings simply cannot do it because as long as we live, we will have a sin nature, which is something within us that gives us a propensity to sin. As long as we have this inner propensity to sin or break God's laws, we will never be perfect in this life.

We cannot one day say "Lord, I promise to stop sinning." If we do that, we are only kidding ourselves and setting ourselves up for major failure. We cannot stop sinning in this life. The most we can do is *want* to stop sinning and then spend the rest of our lives allowing God to create the character of Jesus within us, slowly, little by little.

Repenting is to decide that you no longer want to do the things that keep us out of heaven. We no longer wish to break God's laws. It is not promising God that we will never sin again.

Once we admit, then repent, we must **believe**. This is one of the most difficult things to do because believing that Jesus died in our place, that He lived a perfectly sinless life, is extremely difficult to believe. Our minds cannot grasp that truth. We must ask God to open our eyes to that truth so that we can embrace it.

While on the cross next to Jesus, the one thief joined the other thief in ridiculing Jesus. Then, all of a sudden – as we read in Luke 23 – this same thief that had just been ridiculing Him now turned to Him with a new understanding.

It was this new understanding that prompted the thief to say to Jesus, *"Lord, remember me when you come into your Kingdom."* Jesus looked at the man and responded to him, *"Today, you will be with me in paradise."*

What had occurred in the mind and heart of that thief from one moment to the next? One thing, and that one thing was that God opened the thief's eyes so that he could see the truth. It was as if the blinders fell off and he now saw and understood who Jesus was, even to the most cursory degree that Jesus was dying not for Himself, but for others.

It was this understanding, this awareness, which prompted the man to ask Jesus to simply be remembered. Jesus went way beyond it to promise the man that he would be with Jesus that day in paradise.

Please notice in Luke 23 that there is nothing in the chapter that tells us that the man promised Jesus he would give up sin, or that he would never sin again. There is nothing that tells us that thief took the time to enter into a final deathbed confession of his sins so that he could be absolved.

The thief made no promises to Jesus at all. What he experienced was the truth of who Jesus was and what Jesus accomplished for humanity. Jesus accomplished what we cannot. What is left is for each person to *admit, repent, believe,* and *embrace.*

Let me clarify here that though we do not see any verbal repentance from the thief, we know that he did repent. He admitted as well. How can we know this? It is due to the thief's complete about-face with respect to his attitude toward Jesus. One minute, he was ridiculing Jesus, and the next, embracing Him. This is important. There is no way he could have or would have *embraced* Jesus had he not been humbled by the truth *about* Jesus.

Once the thief saw the truth, he was instantly humbled. Within himself, he knew that he was a sinner, and in fact the text states that this is what he told the other thief dying next to him. *"But the other answering rebuked him, saying, Dost not thou fear God, seeing thou art in the same condemnation? And we indeed justly; for we receive the due reward of our deeds: but this man hath done nothing amiss"* (Luke 23:40-41). Something happened within the heart of the one thief. In one moment, the thief went from harassing Jesus to recognizing his own sinfulness, and then ultimately, asking for grace, which was freely given to him.

Whether he said it or not, the thief went from haughtiness to humility in a very short space of time, and it was all because he saw the truth about Jesus. That truth helped him realize that he deserved his death and what would happen to him after death. He understood that Jesus did not deserve death.

From here, the thief fully embraced the truth about Jesus and was rewarded with eternal life because of it. He did not come off the cross to be water baptized. He did not list a long litany of offenses against God. He recognized the truth about Jesus, was humbled, and embraced that truth!

This is what each of us needs to do. We cannot give in to the lie that tells us that we are not good enough, or we have not given up enough before God will accept us. We must reject the lie that says we must somehow earn our salvation.

Jesus has done everything that is necessary to make salvation available to us. The only thing that is left for us is to see the truth. Once we see that truth, it should humble us to the point of embracing Jesus and all that He stands for and is to us.

The eighth chapter of Romans begins with the fact that all who trust Jesus for salvation are no longer condemned...*ever*. All of my sins – past, present, and future – have not only been forgiven, but canceled. It is because of my faith in the atonement (death) of Jesus that God is able to cancel all of my sins, even the ones that I have not committed yet. This does not make me eager to commit them. It makes me want to do what I can to avoid sinning.

If you do not know Jesus, please do not put down this book without deliberately *believing* that He is God, that He died for you by the shedding of His blood on the cross, and that He rose three days later because death could not keep Him. Do you believe that? If you do not yet believe it, do you *want* to believe it? If so, then simply ask God to help you come to believe all that Jesus is and all that He has accomplished for you. God will answer your prayers and you may either receive instantaneous awareness of all that Jesus is and has done, or it may be a *growing* awareness over time. In either case, it is the most important decision you will ever make.

Turn to Him now and pray for knowledge of the truth and an ability to embrace it. Please. He is waiting for you.

Ask Yourself:

1. Do you *know* Jesus? Are you in *relationship* with Him? Have you had a spiritual transaction according to John 3?
2. Do you *want* to receive eternal life through the only salvation that is available?
3. Do you believe that Jesus is God the Son, who was born of a virgin, lived a sinless life, died a bloody and gruesome death to pay for your sin, was buried, and rose again on the third day? Do you *believe* this?
4. Do you *want* to *embrace* the truth from #3?
5. Pray that God will open your eyes and provide you with the faith to begin believing the truth about Jesus. Ask Him to help your faith embrace the truth, realizing that you are not good enough to save yourself and that your sin will keep you out of God's Kingdom without His salvation.
6. Pray as if your life depended upon it because *it does*!

If you have prayed to receive Jesus as Savior and Lord, please write to me. I want to send you some materials at *no charge or obligation*. Write to me at **fred_deruvo@hotmail.com** and sign up for our free bimonthly newsletter at **www.studygrowknow.com**

RESOURCES

Christian Apologetics:

- *All the Messianic Prophecies of the Bible*
    - Herbert Lockyer (ISBN 0-310-28091-5)0
- *Answering the Objections of Atheists, Agnostics and Skeptics*
    - by Ron Rhodes (ISBN 0-7369-1288-6)
- *Commonly Misunderstood Bible Verses*
    - by Ron Rhodes (ISBN 0-7369-2175-3)
- *Coming to Grips with Genesis*
    - Mortenson & Ury (ISBN 978-0-89051-548-8)
- *Creation and Blessing*
    - Allen P. Ross (ISBN 0-8010-2107-3)
- *Every Prophecy of the Bible*
    - John Walvoord (ISBN1-5647-6758-2)
- *Faith Has Its Reasons*
    - K. Boa & R. Bowman, Jr. (ISBN 1-932805-34-6)
- *Gospel According to Jesus, The*
    - John MacArthur (ISBN 0-310-39491-0)
- *Hell Under Fire*
    - Morgan & Peterson, Editors (ISBN 978-0-3124041-9)
- *Jesus in Context*
    - Bock & Herrick, Editors (ISBN 0-8010-2719-5)
- *Reasons We Believe (50 Lines of Evidence...)*
    - Nathan Busenitz (ISBN 1-4335-0146-5)
- *Six Days of Genesis*
    - Paul F. Taylor (ISBN 978-0-89051-499-3)
- *Stones Cry Out, The*
    - Randall Price (ISBN 978-1-56507-640-2)
- *Temple and Bible Prophecy*
    - Randall Price (ISBN 978-0-73691-387-4)

- *You Can Lead an Atheist to Evidence...*
    - Ray Comfort (ISBN 978-1-935071-06-8)
- *What Does the Bible Say About...?*
    - by Ron Rhodes (ISBN 0-7369-1903-1)

Made in the USA
Charleston, SC
24 October 2011